An Analysis of

Nassim Nicholas Taleb's

The Black Swan:
The Impact of the Highly Improbable

Eric Lybeck

www.macat.com
info@macat.com

Cover illustration: Etienne Gilfillan

Cataloguing in Publication Data
A catalogue record for this book is available from the British Library.
Library of Congress Cataloguing-in-Publication Data is available upon request.

ISBN 978-1-912302-32-1 (hardback)
ISBN 978-1-912128-20-4 (paperback)
ISBN 978-1-912281-20-6 (e-book)

Notice
The information in this book is designed to orientate readers of the work under analysis,
to elucidate and contextualise its key ideas and themes, and to aid in the development
of critical thinking skills. It is not meant to be used, nor should it be used, as a
substitute for original thinking or in place of original writing or research. References and
notes are provided for informational purposes and their presence does not constitute
endorsement of the information or opinions therein. This book is presented solely for
educational purposes. It is sold on the understanding that the publisher is not engaged
to provide any scholarly advice. The publisher has made every effort to ensure that
this book is accurate and up-to-date, but makes no warranties or representations with
regard to the completeness or reliability of the information it contains. The information
and the opinions provided herein are not guaranteed or warranted to produce particular
results and may not be suitable for students of every ability. The publisher shall not be
liable for any loss, damage or disruption arising from any errors or omissions, or from
the use of this book, including, but not limited to, special, incidental, consequential or
other damages caused, or alleged to have been caused, directly or indirectly, by the
information contained within.

CONTENTS

THE MACAT LIBRARY

The Macat Library is a series of unique academic explorations of seminal works in the humanities and social sciences – books and papers that have had a significant and widely recognised impact on their disciplines. It has been created to serve as much more than just a summary of what lies between the covers of a great book. It illuminates and explores the influences on, ideas of, and impact of that book. Our goal is to offer a learning resource that encourages critical thinking and fosters a better, deeper understanding of important ideas.

Each publication is divided into three Sections: Influences, Ideas, and Impact. Each Section has four Modules. These explore every important facet of the work, and the responses to it.

This Section-Module structure makes a Macat Library book easy to use, but it has another important feature. Because each Macat book is written to the same format, it is possible (and encouraged!) to cross-reference multiple Macat books along the same lines of inquiry or research. This allows the reader to open up interesting interdisciplinary pathways.

To further aid your reading, lists of glossary terms and people mentioned are included at the end of this book (these are indicated by an asterisk [*] throughout) – as well as a list of works cited.

Macat has worked with the University of Cambridge to identify the elements of critical thinking and understand the ways in which six different skills combine to enable effective thinking.
Three allow us to fully understand a problem; three more give us the tools to solve it. Together, these six skills make up the **PACIER** model of critical thinking. They are:

ANALYSIS – understanding how an argument is built
EVALUATION – exploring the strengths and weaknesses of an argument
INTERPRETATION – understanding issues of meaning

CREATIVE THINKING – coming up with new ideas and fresh connections
PROBLEM-SOLVING – producing strong solutions
REASONING – creating strong arguments

To find out more, visit **WWW.MACAT.COM.**

CRITICAL THINKING AND *THE BLACK SWAN*

Primary critical thinking skill: CREATIVE THINKING
Secondary critical thinking skill: REASONING

One of the primary qualities of good creative thinking is an intellectual freedom to think outside of the box. Good creative thinkers resist orthodox ideas, take new lines of enquiry, and generally come at problems from the kinds of angles almost no one else could. And, what is more, when the ideas of creative thinkers are convincing, they can reshape an entire topic, and change the orthodoxy for good. Nassim Nicholas Taleb's 2007 bestseller *The Black Swan: The Impact of the Highly Improbable* is precisely such a book: an entertaining, polemical, creative attack on how people in general, and economic experts in particular view the possibility of catastrophic events. Taleb writes with rare creative verve for someone who is also an expert in mathematics, finance, and epistemology (the philosophy of knowledge), and he martials all his skills to turn standard reasoning inside out. His central point is that far from being unimportant, extremely rare events are frequently the most important ones of all: it is highly improbable, highly inconsequential occurrences – what he calls Black Swans – that have shaped history most. As a result, improbability is not a reason to act as if a possible event does not matter, but the opposite.

ABOUT THE AUTHOR OF THE ORIGINAL WORK

Born in 1960, **Nassim Nicholas Taleb** fled a civil war in his native Lebanon and made a fortune as a Wall Street options trader by betting against the market right before the crash of 1987. Those improbable events provide an appropriate backdrop for his most famous book, The Black Swan: The Impact of the Highly Improbable, published in 2007. Taleb quickly became a celebrity after the financial crisis of 2008, which seemed to endorse his view that we shouldn't predict or expect future results based on what has already happened. He continues to participate in the lively debates he touched off in the fields of philosophy, statistics, and economics, among other disciplines.

ABOUT THE AUTHOR OF THE ANALYSIS

Dr Eric Lybeck holds a PhD in sociology from the University of Cambridge and lectures in sociology at the University of Exeter.

ABOUT MACAT

GREAT WORKS FOR CRITICAL THINKING

Macat is focused on making the ideas of the world's great thinkers accessible and comprehensible to everybody, everywhere, in ways that promote the development of enhanced critical thinking skills.

It works with leading academics from the world's top universities to produce new analyses that focus on the ideas and the impact of the most influential works ever written across a wide variety of academic disciplines. Each of the works that sit at the heart of its growing library is an enduring example of great thinking. But by setting them in context – and looking at the influences that shaped their authors, as well as the responses they provoked – Macat encourages readers to look at these classics and game-changers with fresh eyes. Readers learn to think, engage and challenge their ideas, rather than simply accepting them.

'Macat offers an amazing first-of-its-kind tool for interdisciplinary learning and research. Its focus on works that transformed their disciplines and its rigorous approach, drawing on the world's leading experts and educational institutions, opens up a world-class education to anyone.'

Andreas Schleicher
Director for Education and Skills, Organisation for Economic Co-operation and Development

'Macat is taking on some of the major challenges in university education ... They have drawn together a strong team of active academics who are producing teaching materials that are novel in the breadth of their approach.'

Prof Lord Broers,
former Vice-Chancellor of the University of Cambridge

'The Macat vision is exceptionally exciting. It focuses upon new modes of learning which analyse and explain seminal texts which have profoundly influenced world thinking and so social and economic development. It promotes the kind of critical thinking which is essential for any society and economy.
This is the learning of the future.'
Rt Hon Charles Clarke, former UK Secretary of State for Education

'The Macat analyses provide immediate access to the critical conversation surrounding the books that have shaped their respective discipline, which will make them an invaluable resource to all of those, students and teachers, working in the field.'
Professor William Tronzo, University of California at San Diego

WAYS IN TO THE TEXT

KEY POINTS

- Nassim Nicholas Taleb was born in 1960 in Lebanon. He was educated in France and the United States and had a successful career in financial trading before turning his hand to philosophy.*

- His 2007 book *The Black Swan: The Impact of the Highly Improbable* investigates the nature of uncertainty and what happens after highly improbable events that have great consequences.

- The book draws on a number of interrelated disciplines, including higher mathematics and philosophy, to provide a readable understanding of some very complex ideas for a popular audience.

Who Is Nassim Nicholas Taleb?

Nassim Nicholas Taleb, the author of *The Black Swan: The Impact of the Highly Improbable* (2007), was born in 1960 in Amioun, Lebanon—a Middle Eastern country bordered by Syria to the north and east, Israel to the south, and the Mediterranean Sea to the west. He belonged to a respected, well-to-do family with political influence; both his parents were intellectuals. But the family's wealth and power declined when the Lebanese Civil War* broke out unexpectedly in 1975, and Taleb soon left Lebanon to study in France and the United States.

After obtaining a PhD in management science from the University of Paris-Dauphine, Taleb headed back to the United States to become a Wall Street trader.* Given that traders buy and sell stocks with the aim of making a profit, it is essential that they understand and manage a wide variety of risks that can affect prices; Taleb developed new methods and strategies for doing so, and his success made him wealthy.

In the early 2000s, Taleb decided to write books about the philosophical issues surrounding uncertainty—situations in which we make decisions even though the outcome may vary greatly based on factors that are unknown or beyond our control. Taleb had already used his understanding of uncertainty in a positive way in his financial career, but found that the majority of supposed experts— economists,* analysts, statisticians* involved in the analysis of data using numerical representations of things—were still far too willing to trust models that did not account for unpredictable events.

When *The Black Swan* was published in 2007, Taleb became a celebrity overnight. He was invited to give public lectures and keynote speeches, and was regularly asked to comment on world affairs. Everyone wanted to know how to predict the next improbable event. Taleb, however, suggested that people were misunderstanding the point. He emphasized that it is simply not possible to know something before it is known; the Lebanese Civil War, for example, could not have been predicted. We can only know that we do not know everything—and that in itself is an important thing to know.

What Does *The Black Swan* Say?

The Black Swan argues that too often we ignore the possibility that the world around us might change dramatically in the blink of an eye. This is because we rely on induction,* or inductive reasoning: the process via which we predict or expect future results based on the evidence of what has already happened. The term can also can refer to the process of drawing general principles from particular pieces of evidence. For Taleb, induction is a useful form of reasoning, but should be paired with skepticism*—a position of distrust—about declarations of fact. However, since induction can only give us probabilities based on our experiences of the past, this can lead us to believe mistakenly that the future is more certain than it is.

One example of this, from which the book draws its name, is the fact that Europeans once believed that all swans are white. Indeed, whiteness was a defining feature of the very idea of a "swan." Then in the late eighteenth century, a species of black swan was discovered in Australia, and the entire definition of "swan" had to be revised in the light of this new evidence. The discovery of these relatively rare swans was, therefore, both highly improbable and highly consequential.

The story of the black swan shows that while induction can provide conclusions that are *probable* (sometimes, highly probable), those conclusions can radically change if new evidence appears. In this case, induction was not enough to *prove* that no black swans exist. It seemed highly likely, but could never be certain.

Taleb describes this as the asymmetric* quality of evidence. The term "asymmetric" often refers to something that looks different on either side of a central line, but here it has the more specific meaning of "irreversible," or crossing a line that cannot be crossed in reverse. Once black swans were discovered, Europeans could not go back to defining swans as necessarily white.

The story also shows that the absence of evidence is not the same thing as evidence of absence. Just because we have not seen a black swan does not mean that one does not exist somewhere. This, Taleb argues, is a central problem with induction. In many cases, it provides a sensible way of approaching the world and preparing for possible events. But we cannot trust induction completely—although, as Taleb points out, we tend to do exactly that. We become overconfident in our ability to predict the future, and as a result, the negative consequences of Black Swans can be disastrous.

Taleb explains that in our minds, we simplify our experiences into easy categories and we tell ourselves stories to explain them. This leads us to trust in the past, and expect the same in the future. While it is one thing for an individual to do this, Taleb finds it unacceptable when experts in fields such as economics and risk analysis* (a field determining the possibility that a project or endeavor will fail, commonly with considerations of the financial consequences) do the same. He criticizes the ways experts take credit for positive events, while excusing themselves for negative outcomes.

Taleb hopes that by better understanding how Black Swans arise and affect our lives, we might be able to prevent the worst of their negative effects. Further, he wants us to distrust the expertise of those who create a false sense of security, when in reality, anything can happen.

Why Does *The Black Swan* Matter?

The Black Swan introduces the reader to a range of problems related to uncertainty, and points toward potential solutions. These problems include the ways in which unknown phenomena and events often emerge randomly, leading to completely unforeseen—and at times highly dramatic—consequences. The solutions can be hard to find.

Taleb encourages us to adopt new ways of thinking based on his discoveries. His ideas are drawn from a range of complex scientific and philosophical perspectives, which he describes in plain English. He demonstrates that previous knowledge often leads to overconfident predictions that falsely assume that the future will resemble the past. More than this, he demonstrates how experts unconsciously reproduce this error, which further misleads the public. Taleb therefore helps us to understand what is at stake with the problem of induction, while providing us with the means to assess "expert advice" with some hesitation. In short, he helps readers think for themselves through a skeptical approach to received knowledge.

Taleb's book skyrocketed into public awareness after the Black Swan events of the financial crisis of 2008.* In the fall of that year, Lehman Brothers, a large, prestigious financial firm in the US, suddenly filed for bankruptcy. The public and experts were flabbergasted, and worries raised by the event helped launch a global economic downturn that continued for years. While Taleb's ideas cannot explain the crisis itself, they do help explain why virtually no one seemed to see it coming.

Today, Taleb's work continues to influence public debate. His concepts are now being used in a range of disciplines, including organizational science* (the study of human organizations), climate science* (the study of the processes that form the earth's climate), engineering, and statistics. Taleb not only alerts us to issues related to uncertainty, but also provides practical ways to prepare for unexpected outcomes. Regrettably, economists appear to have ignored the bulk of his findings, preferring instead to continue their extended study of the more common—and easily understood—"white swans." *The Black Swan* states that they do this at their own risk.

SECTION 1
INFLUENCES

MODULE 1
THE AUTHOR AND THE
HISTORICAL CONTEXT

KEY POINTS

- *The Black Swan* examines how natural and social events can take us by surprise, with huge consequences.

- Taleb's experiences as a teenager in Lebanon during the Lebanese Civil War,* and later as a trader* on Wall Street buying and selling stocks, led him to recognize the extent to which people fail to expect the unexpected.

- The market crash of October 19, 1987 amplified Taleb's distrust of "expert" predictions, especially those of economists.*

Why Read This Text?

Nassim Nicholas Taleb's *The Black Swan: The Impact of the Highly Improbable* makes a powerful argument about the nature of reality and the ways in which unexpected events and unseen phenomena have a tendency to surprise us. Taleb provides an argument for skepticism:* a call for hesitation before trusting formal models, either in our own minds or from the minds of "experts."

Taleb uses familiar examples, told in an understandable style, to explain how extremely unlikely yet highly consequential events (events with significant consequences) may upend our sense of reality at any given moment. As he points out, it is not expected events that change the course of human history, but unexpected events. Indeed, if we think about it, he writes, "A small number of Black Swans explain almost everything in our world, from the

> **❝** The Lebanese 'paradise' suddenly evaporated, after a few bullets and mortar shells ... After close to thirteen centuries of remarkable coexistence, a Black Swan, coming out of nowhere, transformed the place from heaven to hell. **❞**
>
> Nassim Nicholas Taleb, *The Black Swan: The Impact of the Highly Improbable*

success of ideas and religions, to the dynamics of historical events, to elements of our own personal lives."[1]

Because the book was published just ahead of the financial crisis of 2008,* it was thereafter promoted as a "prediction" of what was to come. The book has been heavily discussed in popular, professional, and academic contexts.

Author's Life

Taleb grew up in Lebanon, a Middle Eastern country that borders the eastern edge of the Mediterranean Sea. His grandfather was an important civil servant, and his family—descended from Greek Orthodox Christians—were members of an educated, intellectual middle class. Taleb attended an elite French *lyceé* (secondary school) and studied philosophy,* languages, and mathematics. By 15, he had become something of a rebel and was jailed during a student riot in which he (allegedly) attacked a policeman. While many of his friends denied their participation in the student movement, Taleb spoke out freely about it. This attitude actually raised Taleb's status within his intellectual and respectable family. "My paternal uncle was not too bothered by my political ideas (these come and go); he was outraged that I used them as an excuse to dress sloppily,"[2] Taleb wrote.

Only a few months later, the 1975 Lebanese Civil War broke out and the stable world that Taleb and his community had always known was upended forever. Christians and Muslims had lived in peace there for centuries, but after a period of low-level tension they suddenly took to arms and began a bitter fight. The civil war lasted for 17 years.

Taleb's experience in Lebanon demonstrated that unexpected events could have monumental consequences. He remained deeply affected by the start of a war that very few had predicted.

During this long conflict, Taleb left Lebanon, along with many other members of the intellectual middle class. He studied business at Wharton School in Philadelphia and later obtained a PhD in management science from the University of Paris-Dauphine. Although Taleb's intellectual interests lay in philosophy, he became a financial trader on Wall Street. There he helped to develop a range of innovative financial instruments (in the form of tradable assets, which can even be things such as the debt held by companies or individuals) that are used to reduce and manage the risk of losing money.

Author's Background

During a conversation with an (unidentified) Italian philosopher, Taleb had discovered someone who similarly emphasized the role of chance in real-life events. This philosopher insisted, however, that Taleb could not have, and would not have, developed his ideas had he been raised in a Protestant household (Protestantism being one of the two principal branches of the Christian faith). Although Taleb does not make the Italian's reasoning clear, his point is that he sought a simple explanation or cause for Taleb's ideas by looking at his upbringing in the Orthodox Church.[3] Taleb would suggest that this is an example of the "narrative fallacy:"* an attempt to understand the roots of an idea within a wider context by making a plausible "story" about it in retrospect.

Despite Taleb's dismissal of the idea, it is highly probable that the chaotic context of his early adulthood had a strong influence on his thinking. The Lebanese war was as extreme as it was unanticipated, forever disrupting the lives of millions, including Taleb's family. The Wall Street crash of 1987* was another likely influence, causing what at the time was the largest financial crisis since the catastrophic economic collapse of the late 1920s and 1930s known as the Great Depression. This event was completely unforeseen and unexpected by virtually all professional and academic experts. Taleb had been one of the only analysts to anticipate a crash; he made a large investment that enabled him to profit from it, and the experience justified his criticism of Wall Street's overconfidence. "It was hard to tell my friends, all hurt in some manner by the crash, about this feeling of vindication."[4]

The war in Lebanon and his experience on Wall Street in 1987 seem to have taught Taleb that the one thing he could say for certain was that he could not be too sure of anything.

NOTES

1   Nassim Nicholas Taleb, *The Black Swan: The Impact of the Highly Improbable* (London: Penguin, 2008), xxii.

2   Taleb, *Black Swan*, 6.

3   Taleb, *Black Swan*, 62.

4   Taleb, *Black Swan*, 21.

MODULE 2
ACADEMIC CONTEXT

KEY POINTS

- Taleb's work is interdisciplinary: it draws on the aims and methods of statistics,* economics,* and philosophy,* disciplines that aim to predict future outcomes using models based on past history.

- Economics and statistics are characterized by mathematical rigor and a hesitancy to make predictions without sufficient data. As a result, unexpected phenomena are regularly excluded from their models.

- Taleb's successes as a financial trader* gave him both financial and intellectual freedom; he has used this to challenge the central assumptions used by various disciplines to make predictions.

The Work in its Context

Nassim Nicholas Taleb's *The Black Swan: The Impact of the Highly Improbable* challenges several intellectual disciplines at once. He argues that the central assumptions of statistics, economics, finance,* and social science all fail to account sufficiently for the likelihood of highly unpredictable events.

At root, Taleb addresses the problem of epistemology,* a branch of philosophy that asks "How do we know what we know?" His argument builds on the work of earlier philosophers who believed, simply, that we do not know as much as we think we know.[1]

Taleb's criticisms are directed largely at the misuse of philosophical models within professionally-oriented fields like finance and economics.

66 Somehow you have a lot of ideas, but they do not seem connected; the logic linking them remains concealed to you. Meanwhile ... blue collars of the thinking business tell you that you are too spread out between fields; you reply that these disciplines are artificial and arbitrary, to no avail. **99**

Nassim Nicholas Taleb, *The Black Swan: The Impact of the Highly Improbable*

Overview of the Field

Taleb's central topic—the problem of induction,* or making future predictions based on the evidence of past events—has a long history within philosophy. At a basic level, induction raises the question as to how and when we can generalize from a limited range of data. While there are ancient examples of scholars who addressed similar questions, Taleb's more recent philosophical predecessors include the eighteenth-century Scottish philosopher David Hume* and the twentieth-century German philosopher Karl Popper.*

Hume developed an empiricist* perspective on knowledge, which means he believed that the experience of our senses is the most important basis for acquiring knowledge. He distinguished between "matters of fact" and "relations of ideas." Matters of fact are "falsifiable," in that a statement such as "all swans are white" can be disproven by new factual evidence. Relational ideas, on the other hand, are things like "2+2=4." This is true because of the way "2" and "4" are defined, so it cannot be disproven by new evidence.

Hume's groundbreaking work changed the way philosophers thought about cause and effect, no longer seeing them as forces objectively present in nature. Rather, Hume argued that our experience of cause and effect is a reflection of our expectations.

Popper's contribution to inductive philosophy similarly challenged the existing notions of his day, at a time when philosophers were preoccupied with logical positivism.* Positivism had suggested that the only truths were those aspects of reality that could be measured and empirically verified. Popper suggested that *verification* is not enough for establishing truth; for him, empirical statements deemed "true" must be *falsifiable*: that is, capable of being proven wrong.

The empiricist tradition had a long history in philosophy, and Popper's falsificationism* became important within the philosophy of science. However, within twentieth-century Anglo-American academia, analytic philosophy* became the most influential philosophical school. The analytic school was very formal, and focused on logic, relationships, and the definition of terms; it asserted that there was such a thing as a "right" way of thinking. Taleb rejected this view.

Academic Influences

The fields of statistics, economics, and finance draw on the principle of induction, seeking to make predictions from patterns of past events. One of the models they use is known as a Gaussian* or "bell" curve, a distribution of outcomes that frequently corresponds to reality. A bell curve is a graph shaped like a bell, with the largest number of results clustered near the middle, or average. The graph tapers down to the left and right for results higher and lower than the average, and flattens out at the extremes of high and low.[2]

As a simple example of the concept of a bell curve, imagine rolling two dice. The possible totals range from 2 to 12, with 2 and 12 as the least likely outcomes, because there is only one combination of the two dice that will return each of those results. The most likely outcome is 7, as six combinations give that result (1+6, 2+5, 3+4, 4+3, 5+2, 6+1). The second most likely outcomes are 6 and 8, and the likelihood continues to decline in each direction. (This example is so simple that the graph would decline in a straight line rather than a curve, but it shows how the average, most likely results are in the middle, while the extreme, least likely results are at the far left and right.)

Based on the insights of Hume, Popper, and others, Taleb argues that bell curves and similar models do not adequately account for improbable but significant events. For instance, while 12 and 2 are the *least likely* totals for two dice, they might be the *most decisive* rolls in terms of winning or losing a given game. Taleb therefore draws on alternative forms of mathematical and philosophical understanding.

One influence is the concept of "fractals"* in the field of geometry, developed in the late twentieth century by the French American mathematician Benoit Mandelbrot.*[3] "Fractal" refers to a pattern that repeats itself indefinitely. As an example, consider how a tree grows. The tree trunk starts as a small stem emerging from a seed in the ground. As it grows, the trunk begins to send out branches in different directions. As the branches grow, they send out their own branches, which send out *their* own branches. This process could theoretically continue forever, although in reality a tree has size limits. (There are mathematical fractals, however, that are truly infinite.) Taleb drew on fractal geometry to explain why unexpected events can lead to extreme outcomes that cannot be described by the familiar bell curve model.

Similarly, modern philosophy's "chaos theory"* asserts that even a tiny disturbance—for example, a butterfly flapping its wings—can generate a considerable weather event far away. Chaos theory recognizes that in actively changing systems, although initial conditions may be known, the possible outcomes of a process can vary so widely that they might as well be random—that is, unpredictable.[4] The world, simply, is less stable and predictable than traditional scholars can account for using the airtight logic of the analytic philosophers and mathematical modelers.

NOTES

1   David Hume, *A Treatise of Human Nature: Being an Attempt to Introduce the Experimental Method of Reasoning into Moral Subjects* (Oxford: Oxford University Press, 2000); Karl Popper, *The Logic of Scientific Discovery* (London: Routledge, 2002).

2   Ian Hacking, *Logic of Statistical Inference* (Cambridge: Cambridge University Press, 1965).

3   Benoit Mandelbrot, *The Fractal Geometry of Nature* (San Francisco: W.H. Freeman and Co., 1982).

4   Francis Moon, *Chaotic and Fractal Dynamics* (New York: Wiley, 1992).

MODULE 3
THE PROBLEM

KEY POINTS

- While Taleb's argument about the importance of the improbable was not new to the discipline of philosophy,* the concept had failed to translate into practice in statistics,* economics,* and finance.*

- Meanwhile, in fractal* geometry—a new field of mathematics interested in repeated patterns, attention to chaos,* and uncertainty—the assumption of "normality" as the default condition or expectation was being superseded.

- Taleb, who did not belong to any particular academic discipline, drew on his experience as a Wall Street trader,* where he analyzed financial data to assess investment risk. He demonstrated that any model that did not account for the possibility of rapid unexpected change from a single event was flawed.

Core Question

In *The Black Swan: The Impact of the Highly Improbable*, Nassim Nicholas Taleb is interested in resolving the "problem of induction."* Unlike deductive* reasoning, which assumes certain things to be true before exploring and explaining reality, inductivism seeks to prove a claim of truth. Deductive reasoning works from known premises toward logically certain claims; inductive reasoning works from evidence towards probable claims. For example, one might deduce: "All men die. I am a man. Therefore I will die." For an inductivist, new evidence or a change in conditions could overthrow the validity of

> ❝ The traditional Gaussian way of looking at the
> world begins by focusing on the ordinary, and
> then deals with exceptions or so called outliers as
> ancillaries. But there is a second way, which takes
> the exceptional as a starting point and treats the
> ordinary as subordinate. ❞
>
> Nassim Nicholas Taleb, *The Black Swan: The Impact of the Highly Improbable*

the original claim. In a world of Black Swans, these truth claims can
be upended at any time. Just because things have been one way does
not mean they will remain that way.

Philosophy recognizes the limitations of making general claims
based on data that is not complete. Taleb, though, is interested
in why more people in the wider world do not recognize this
fact more often. In our daily lives, in politics, and especially in
economic markets, significant yet unexpected events often occur.
And yet "experts" and forecasters continue to apply models based
on "normal" events, which distort our perceptions and give false
confidence in a stable, predictable future. Taleb's question is, "Why
don't we learn from our mistakes?"

The Participants

The notion that unexpected events can surprise us, triggering
upheaval of our existing sense of reality, has long been known to
philosophers. This was the problem of induction identified by
scholars, including the Scottish philosopher David Hume* and the
German philosopher Karl Popper.*¹ These scholars described a range
of generalizations that were "asymmetric,"* or irreversible. Even if we
are completely confident in our sense of a given phenomenon—for
example, if we are confident that all swans are white—it would take
only a single observation of a black swan to require a revision of what

we define as a swan. This is "asymmetric" because it takes only a single counterexample to disprove conclusions reached from a vast number of consistent examples.

For Taleb, the main participants in the debate about induction were not academics, but practitioners in the world of finance. Financial predictions can have outcomes similar to the real-life Black Swan case: one "outlier"* (an unpredictable, very high, or very low result) can make or lose millions. Financial and economic models are regularly wrong in their predictions because they assume patterns of relatively "normal distributions"—that is, results without major, important outliers beyond the scope of the model.

Within statistics, this normal distribution is called the "Gaussian bell curve"* named after Carl Friedrich Gauss,* a German mathematician who invented this statistical technique in the early nineteenth century. A great deal of statistical work is based on applying a Gaussian curve to observed phenomena. However, as Taleb explains, "the monstrosity called the Gaussian Bell Curve is not Gauss's doing."[2] The idea that historical averages of population or social statistics can provide accurate insights into how future events will unfold arose only when the bell curve was applied by social scientists like Adolph Quetelet,* a nineteenth-century Belgian.

This notion of prediction is most problematic in finance. Taleb criticizes Robert C. Merton* and Myron Scholes,* the American economists who developed investment theories based on formulas for predicting financial risk. Their work brought the Gaussian curve into a range of activities for which it was inapplicable.[3] Financial markets in fact often encounter Black Swan outliers. Despite receiving the Nobel Prize in 1997 for their work, Merton and Scholes's investment fund, Long-Term Capital Management, collapsed in 1998, almost taking the entire financial system with it. As Taleb explains, "Since their models ruled out the possibility of large deviations, they allowed themselves to take a monstrous amount of risk."[4]

The Contemporary Debate

Instead of a Gaussian approach to probability, Taleb draws on an alternative tradition of mathematics derived from the fractal geometry of Benoit Mandelbrot,* a mathematician who worked for years at IBM (and thus outside academia). Fractals sometimes can and do resemble the Gaussian curve, but, at other levels and scales, sharp differences can emerge.

Though Taleb takes on a range of different disciplines at once, many of his central claims are accepted by practicing academics. For example, within statistics, the Gaussian or "normal" distribution is understood to be one of many possible distributions. The relevant kind of distribution needs to be confirmed before analysis can proceed. For Taleb, the problem is the too-hasty application of these ideas and models to the fields of finance and economics.

In 2008, the financial crisis* proved that Taleb was not simply arguing for the sake of argument. Black Swan events really do happen, and in the case of the financial crisis, no one was prepared.

NOTES

1   David Hume, *A Treatise of Human Nature: Being an Attempt to Introduce the Experimental Method of Reasoning into Moral Subjects* (Oxford: Oxford University Press, 2000); Karl Popper, *The Logic of Scientific Discovery* (London: Routledge. 2002).

2   Nassim Nicholas Taleb, *The Black Swan: The Impact of the Highly Improbable* (London: Penguin, 2008), 241.

3   Roger Lowenstein, *When Genius Failed: The Rise and Fall of Long-Term Capital Management* (New York: Random House, 2000).

4   Taleb, *Black Swan*, 282.

MODULE 4
THE AUTHOR'S CONTRIBUTION

KEY POINTS

- Taleb is interested in explaining why experts reproduce the common mental biases that prevent us from recognizing the natural unpredictability of the world.

- Taleb challenges central assumptions within fields as different as statistics,* economics,* and philosophy.* He demands that we take seriously risks that are unaccounted for in traditional forms of knowing.

- While many scholars in these fields have put forward similar arguments, few have done so with such consistency and with such insistence. While we know intellectually that unpredictable events may influence reality, why do our mathematical models reflect a more stable world?

Author's Aims

Nassim Nicholas Taleb's *The Black Swan: The Impact of the Highly Improbable* focuses on the failure of disciplines such as economics, finance,* sociology,* and philosophy to realize a simple truth: sometimes, reality hits us unexpectedly with a dramatic, unforeseen event that has tremendous consequences. These events happen often, whether in the financial crises of 1987* or 2008,* or in wars that arise from seemingly nowhere. World War I* and the Lebanese Civil War* are two examples repeatedly cited by Taleb.

Yet these academic disciplines pretend they can construct models of reality based on past information as if the future will be the same as the past. This implies a stable present that no change can dramatically

> ❝ Almost all the history of thought is about what we know, or think we know. *The Black Swan* is the very first attempt (that I know of) in the history of thought to provide a map of where we get hurt by what we don't know, to set systematic limits to the fragility of knowledge—and to provide exact locations where these maps no longer work. ❞
>
> Nassim Nicholas Taleb, *The Black Swan: The Impact of the Highly Improbable*

disrupt. Taleb tries to show that in all forms of knowledge we must take the idea of contingency* seriously, meaning that unexpected events can undermine or disprove theories that are widely accepted as truth. He asks two questions: First, how significant are unforeseen events and where do they tend to occur? Second, where and why do certain ways of thinking prevent us from recognizing or preparing for these events? In so doing, he turns philosophical problems into more practical questions about what we should actually do about it, and why we have not acted already.

Taleb manages to restate the problem in ways that are highly accessible to the intelligent reader, while also being technically rigorous. He preempts a range of criticisms and forces critics and scholars in various fields onto his own turf. He frames the question of induction*—the search for evidence to support a theory—so thoroughly that readers meet Taleb at least halfway. We stop asking for further justification of the notion that the unexpected can be important, and start asking, "Why did we not see this earlier, and more clearly?"

Approach

The Black Swan creates the impression that Taleb spends every minute of every day obsessing over the range of concerns documented in his book. There is no overarching, systematic, or formal approach to the questions he considers; rather, he has developed his own particular way of thinking. Though he uses data, theories, and insights from philosophy, mathematics, and financial theory, Taleb's central tactic is to use stories and analogies to support his points and persuade the reader. As he suggests, since economics and financial forecasting are "narrative disciplines" his "best tool [to counter them] is a narrative." After all, he continues, "Ideas come and go, stories stay."[1] In writing this way, Taleb reproduces the experience of relating inductively and skeptically* to uncertainty. He gets the reader to see the world as he sees it.

What emerges from his writings, then, is a new way of seeing familiar intellectual arenas—including statistics, economics, and professional activities such as finance. These are areas in which highly contingent and unexpected events occur regularly. Yet the prevailing models and approaches of these disciplines continue to reflect an assumed stability and consistency—which is wholly inappropriate.

By training readers' minds to think differently, Taleb brings us into his camp, where we can no longer take the organized opinions of economists very seriously. He puts the burden on them to demonstrate why we should assume a normal course of events, when a perfect example of such normality never appears to exist. By returning to the question of how we know what we know, and by mapping the limits of knowledge, Taleb addresses widespread academic concerns about assumptions that go unchallenged despite their blatant flaws.

Contribution in Context

Taleb's main contribution to the debate around induction is to synthesize the different academic approaches with his experience as a trader and make use of several currents of thought that were brewing when he began working on Wall Street. These include the emergence of "chaos theory"* and fractal* geometry as developed by the Polish

French mathematician Benoit Mandelbrot.* "Wars," Taleb writes, "are fractal in nature—meaning there is no limit to how large they can be. A war that kills more people than the devastating Second World War* is possible, although such a war is unlikely and has never happened in the past."[2] While these perspectives were known, they were not yet commonly discussed in academia; as a result, various outdated assumptions still held sway regarding the nature of reality.

In economics, for example, statistics were regularly deployed to predict the future based on past data. But what if an unexpected downturn or transition within the market occurred? If these events were predictable, they would already be incorporated in the model. In reality, one unexpected event could dramatically upend and ultimately invalidate existing models and predictions.

Taleb uses many examples to demonstrate just how far this tendency goes. He shows how common it is to trust in the stability of the future, and how dangerous this assumption can be. For example, consider the devastation wreaked in the United States by Hurricane Katrina* in 2005. While American cities had prepared for hurricanes in the past, no one expected an event of such magnitude in a city as vulnerable as New Orleans. Consequently, the population suffered as much from the ill-planned and ineffective early responses as from the storm itself.

NOTES

1   Nassim Nicolas Taleb, *The Black Swan: The Impact of the Highly Improbable* (London: Penguin, 2008), xxvii.

2   Taleb, *Black Swan*, 271.

MODULE 5
MAIN IDEAS

KEY POINTS

- Taleb's *Black Swan* deals with three themes: the problem associated with inductive* reasoning; the mental tricks humans play on themselves because they trust such reasoning; and the problems these misjudgments create for so-called "experts" in their fields.

- Taleb argues that we should pay more attention to Black Swans: entirely unexpected events that have profound consequences. Such events have transformative possibilities that experts and society should prepare for and use to their advantage.

- *Black Swan* is written for a general audience as well as for academics; it combines stylish storytelling and elements of fiction with more complex technical prose.

Key Themes

Nassim Nicholas Taleb's *The Black Swan: The Impact of the Highly Improbable* is an examination of how completely unexpected phenomena affect humans, how we might and should account for them, and how we can seize on the possibilities they offer. The concept of the Black Swan is drawn from the example of the deductive* statement "all swans are white" made famous by the German philosopher* Karl Popper.* Because all swans observed by Europeans were white, people deduced that swans, in general, were always white. However, the discovery of a black swan in Australia in the eighteenth century instantly and permanently falsified (that is, revealed to be false) this deduced statement. Europeans had to revise their definition

> **❝** Almost everything in social life is produced by rare but consequential shocks and jumps; all the while almost everything studied about social life focuses on the 'normal'. **❞**
>
> Nassim Nicholas Taleb, *The Black Swan: The Impact of the Highly Improbable.*

and expectations of what was meant by a "swan." As Taleb notes, "One single observation can invalidate a general statement derived from millennia of confirmatory sightings of millions of white swans."[1]

Taleb's point is simple: a broad collection of data confirming a condition to be true under many circumstances is not enough to prove it cannot be made untrue. Reality has a tendency to surprise us.

For Taleb, Black Swan names the entire range of unexpected phenomena that generate profound and consequential effects. These occur often enough for us to need to be wary of them; but because of the way our minds work, we are rarely sufficiently prepared for them.

This blind spot is reinforced by the unreliability of "experts" who offer us predictions based on formal models. Taleb roundly criticizes a range of academic disciplines and professional fields, especially finance,* which are prone to error when the random nature of the world is ignored.

Instead of ignoring Black Swans, Taleb argues that we should expect some sort of unexpected events to occur, even if we cannot know specifically what they might be. We can achieve this defense against Black Swans through a form of inductive skepticism:* seeking tangible evidence to reveal flaws in our assumptions whenever possible, rather than just looking for evidence to support a model. By acknowledging the limitations of our own knowledge, we can counteract some of the worst effects of Black Swans and potentially turn them into what Taleb calls "Gray Swans"*—extreme events that can be modeled.[2]

Exploring the Ideas

Taleb engages with the age-old limitations of induction: How can we derive understandings of phenomena we have *not* observed by using information about things we *have* observed? In other words, what is the correct level of generalization to be gained from observation? The example of a discovery of black swans in Australia reflects an "asymmetry"* of proof: many observations of white swans are not enough to prove that all swans truly are white—a single observation of a black swan disproves the theory.

He uses the simple example of a turkey that is fed every day. "Every single feeding will firm up the bird's belief that is it is the general rule of life to be fed every day by friendly members of the human race."[3] Then, at Thanksgiving, that assumption is overturned. "The turkey problem can be generalized to any situation where the same hand that feeds you can be the one that wrings your neck."[4]

Taleb relates the limitations of induction to a range of cognitive fallacies* that humans constantly repeat (a cognitive fallacy is when our minds convince us of something that may not be true, based on a misunderstanding or on incomplete information.) Finally, he demonstrates the way these fallacies are embedded within the logic of a range of scientific disciplines. Scientists, professionals, and philosophers regularly fail to deal with the limitations of induction, resulting in terrible and potentially harmful predictions and actions.

Taleb notes that Black Swans are real. There are countless examples, from an unexpected stock market crash to World War I,* which have fundamentally changed the way society looks at reality. Because of the scale and significance of the changes that often follow Black Swans, we cannot explain away or ignore these events as "unlikely" or "irrelevant." They are significant precisely *because* we do not know a Black Swan until we see one.

Yet this fallacy is precisely what we tend to act on, due to the way we process knowledge and the nature of Black Swans themselves—

since, by definition, they are unexpected. They are so rare that we tell ourselves they will not come any time soon, if at all. In fact, our brains are structured to encourage the simplification of complex information, and we would not be able to function without some notion of stability. "The same condition that makes us simplify pushes us to think that the world is less random than it actually is,"[5] Taleb writes.

Taleb reserves considerable criticism for supposedly "scientific" and "advanced" forms of knowledge that claim to predict the future. According to him, economists,* sociologists,* and "skilled" professionals who claim to know the future—such as financial traders*—are no better than soothsayers or fortune-tellers.

Language and Expression

As philosophy texts go, *Black Swan* is a relatively easy read. Taleb begins with a range of literary examples to introduce the central idea he wants the reader to understand. He travels through autobiographical and fictional examples, then uses these as a basis for the technical explanation of his ideas. He always retains a familiar style, with humor and the regular use of grounded examples.

The book is not a sustained, step-by-step argument, but rather the unfolding of an idea: the limitations of induction and its consequences. The idea, in fact, is relatively simple, though it is possible to "get it" without fully understanding how and where his argument works.

Taleb therefore communicates the Black Swan idea in every comprehensible way, using stories, examples (both real and fictional), technical explanations, glossaries, and so on. Because of his style and willingness to lay out his points from so many angles and in so many ways, the book became a major best seller with a wide readership. This popular appeal should not be confused with a lack of rigor, however, for the book has challenged the assumptions of experts in a range of fields—precisely as Taleb intended.

NOTES

1 Nassim Nicholas Taleb, *The Black Swan: The Impact of the Highly Improbable* (London: Penguin, 2008), xxi.

2 Taleb, *Black Swan*, 272.

3 Taleb, *Black Swan*, 40.

4 Taleb, *Black Swan*, 40.

5 Taleb, *Black Swan*, 69.

MODULE 6
SECONDARY IDEAS

KEY POINTS

- Taleb wants us to recognize that improbable or unexpected events occur more often than we think, and that we should be alert to them. He wants us to understand why experts seem to systematically avoid this recognition.

- Taleb takes on a number of disciplines at once, challenging the central assumptions of statistical,* economic,* and philosophical* knowledge.

- Economics, the discipline Taleb challenges most directly, has adapted the least to his criticism. Statistics, on the other hand, has entered a dialogue and appears to have incorporated Taleb's suggestions to some extent, in both pure and applied mathematics.

Other Ideas

In addition to introducing the notion of Black Swans, in *The Black Swan: The Impact of the Highly Improbable* Nassim Nicholas Taleb encourages us to realize how often we talk ourselves out of understanding these unpredictable phenomena. Our minds, he notes, tend toward simplifications. One way we do this is via the "narrative fallacy":* the way in which we tell ourselves narratives, or stories, about the past and future.[1] Once we accept the narrative, we tend to disregard any evidence against it. This problem is compounded by the mental connection between causality* (the actual causes of events) and narrativity* (what seems to make sense as a "story" about such causes). As Taleb explains, "Narrativity can viciously

> ❝ *The Black Swan* is about consequential epistemic* limitations, both psychological (hubris* and biases) and philosophical (mathematical) limits to knowledge, both individual and collective ... So *The Black Swan* is about human error in some domains, swelled by a long tradition of scientism* and a plethora of information that fuels confidence without increasing knowledge. ❞
>
> Nassim Nicholas Taleb, *The Black Swan: The Impact of the Highly Improbable*

affect the remembrance of past events as follows: we will tend to more easily remember those facts from our past that fit a narrative, while we tend to neglect others that do not appear to play a causal role in that narrative."[2]

This is a problem we all face: we try to simplify our understanding of the world around us. So we tend to focus on dramatic events and probabilities—things such as terrorism, which are extremely unlikely to affect us as individuals. Meanwhile we focus less on repeated phenomena, the causes of which could be more widely recognized if thought about correctly. Taleb emphasizes the Black Swans that we do *not* expect as much as the high-profile Black Swans that we *do* expect, but which never arrive.

These observations may tell us something about the way our minds work, but as ordinary people we may not be capable of changing. The real problem, for Taleb, arises when experts claim to rise above these natural-born limitations, proclaiming an ability to model the past, present, and future accurately. Taleb invents a term for this, calling it the "ludic fallacy,"* from the Latin word for "game." The ludic fallacy is when experts believe that their models and predictions resemble the calculable odds in regulated games, such as those in a casino. In fact, a world with Black Swans operates without any such regularized odds. In the real world, the odds are constantly shifting beneath our feet.

Yet, so-called experts in finance* and economics provide us with "measurements" of risk, based on the assumption that past patterns and conditions will remain stable now and into the future. They maintain faith in probabilities based on this assumption, despite its major failures in the past, such as the stock market and economic crashes of 1987* and 2008.* The experts, who did not see these events coming, then revise their stories to demonstrate their underlying causes. With this in hand they offer us new models, while remaining unprepared for a future Black Swan event.

Taleb concludes by offering strategies to reduce the worst effects of Black Swans, trying to convert them into what he calls "Gray Swans:"* extreme events that can be modeled, and which may result in less extreme consequences.

Exploring the Ideas

Taleb is as much interested in why we so rarely recognize Black Swans as he is in Black Swans themselves: he reflects on how our minds prevent us from living in a world full of such uncertainty. We can, however, potentially avoid these flawed ways of thinking by treating the world around us with skepticism.* Rather than trusting our instincts, we can test and refine our knowledge of the world through experience.

One particular bias we usually retain is confirmation bias:* that is, looking for evidence to support our theory or point of view, rather than information that might disprove it. Referencing empiricism,* the principle of basing analysis on verifiable evidence, Taleb writes, "By a mechanism I call naïve empiricism, we have a natural tendency to look for instances that confirm our story and our vision of the world—these instances are always easy to find ... You take past instances that corroborate your theories and you treat them as evidence."[3]

The problem is that there is no such thing as conclusive evidence when reality is structured "asymmetrically."* In other words, the observer can prove that most of the known results fall within a range that is considered "normal" or expected, but cannot prove that there are no profound "outliers,"* or results far outside the normal range.

The effect of this is that we can know with greater assurance that a statement is wrong than we can know that it is right. And, yet, within prediction-making disciplines including economics and finance, models are promoted with irrational confidence. These models are not sufficiently prepared for Black Swans.

Taleb does not suggest that "all is random" or that there is no point in predicting the future—provided these predictions are realistic and do not overly assume "normality" and stability. He discusses how to deal with "Gray Swans" based on fractal geometry,* where infinitely repeating patterns show that extreme results are possible. As he puts it, this allows a certain amount of preparedness for shocking events: "You are indeed much safer if you know where the wild animals are."[4]

Overlooked

Certainly the discipline that has done the least to account for Taleb's ideas is economics, even though this was the field most directly challenged by the argument at the heart of the book. Related disciplines such as statistics and philosophy were more willing to engage with his work. Notions such as the asymmetry of causation are not sufficiently understood outside philosophy, which can have disastrous consequences. Even some critics of Taleb's work seemed grateful to have found in him an excellent spokesperson for inductive* skepticism.

Taleb suggests that the mathematical models used by economists are no better than some soothsayers' predictions, derived from the primitive rituals of ancient times. The field of economics, however, has not reformed itself as a result of his ideas. This neglect is unfortunate, for in many instances Taleb offers ways to predict without distorting, by accounting for a reality filled with Black Swans. He has developed this work further in subsequent texts.[5] In the future, as this more recent technical work filters through related disciplines, the field of economic and financial prediction may catch up with Taleb's work by recognizing the inherent limitations of any predictive model.

NOTES

1   Daniel Kahneman and Amos Tversky, "On the Reality of Cognitive Illusions," *Psychological Review* 103 (1996): 582–91.

2   Nassim Nicholas Taleb, *The Black Swan: The Impact of the Highly Improbable* (London: Penguin, 2008), 70.

3   Taleb, *Black Swan*, 55.

4   Taleb, *Black Swan*, 272.

5   Nassim Nicholas Taleb, *Antifragile: Things That Gain from Disorder* (London: Penguin, 2012); Nassim Nicholas Taleb, "Errors, Robustness, and the Fourth Quadrant," *International Journal of Forecasting* 25, no. 4 (2009): 744–59; Nassim Nicholas Taleb and Constantine Sandis, "The Skin In The Game Heuristic for Protection Against Tail Events," *Review of Behavioral Economics* 1 (2014): 1–21.

MODULE 7
ACHIEVEMENT

KEY POINTS

- Taleb's goal was to make readers realize that the possibility of a "highly improbable consequential event" was significant and worthy of our attention. After the financial collapse of 2008,* he certainly got our attention.

- Historical circumstances played a role in introducing Taleb's message to a wide audience, but he helped by writing in a colloquial and anecdotal style (informal, and narratively oriented), making it accessible to an intelligent, educated readership.

- While Taleb's argument continues to make headway within some intellectual disciplines, perhaps his most central target—economics*—has yet to take the full weight of his ideas seriously.

Assessing the Argument

In *The Black Swan: The Impact of the Highly Improbable*, Nassim Nicholas Taleb sought to provide a philosophical justification for his time-tested perspective on the financial markets. He had learned at an early age to be prepared for the unknown and unexpected, and brought this to bear in his work as a trader* in the financial markets of Wall Street. He developed robust investment systems that protected him against most forms of unexpected behavior, while remaining open to certain opportunities with low risk and high returns. This contributed to a financial career consisting of long dry spells interrupted by periodic windfalls.

This success contributed to a growing confidence in his approach,

> **❝** The idea is not to correct mistakes and eliminate randomness from social and economic life through monetary policy, subsidies, and so on. The idea is simply to let human mistakes and miscalculations remain confined and to prevent their spreading through the system. **❞**
>
> Nassim Nicholas Taleb, *The Black Swan: The Impact of the Highly Improbable*

but still Taleb could not adequately express precisely how and why he did what he did. Explaining the Black Swan was part of an obsessive quest for self-discovery as much as anything else. He did not have anything particular to prove to any academic discipline, since he had never been a professional philosopher* or even a professional economist. In *Fooled by Randomness*, originally published in 2001, Taleb discussed many of these ideas in print.[1] However, he still wanted to outline rigorously the philosophical basis for his ideas, and in 2007 *The Black Swan* was intended to do so. The book quickly became a best seller after the financial crisis of 2008, which launched Taleb into a mass-market category that includes social scientists and philosophers such as Malcolm Gladwell,* author of *The Tipping Point*, and Thomas Friedman,* who writes on global affairs.

This was both a blessing and a curse for Taleb, who had thought he was writing a fully comprehensive book. The argument reached a wide audience across a range of fields, but many did not recognize the book's technical qualities. Taleb believed these scholars missed the forest for the trees, perhaps because of his familiar, storytelling writing style.

Taleb has spent subsequent years writing more technical papers, continually updating and refining his arguments. While the core of these ideas is present in *The Black Swan*, his later literature made it more immediately evident.

Taleb was able to think in untraditional ways, or "outside the box," because of his independence from existing intellectual disciplines. Yet in the long run he seems to have benefited from participation in academic discussions, which have helped him further develop his ideas.

Achievement in Context

It is worth noting that there is little fundamentally new within Taleb's argument. That said, his wide-ranging influences, along with his (self-proclaimed) outsider status in relation to the academic world, allow him to express the limitations of induction* in a fresh and engaging way. It is an old problem, in which we are given the responsibility for checking our assumptions against testable, observable evidence. We should seek to challenge those assumptions rather than accept beliefs because they have yet to be disproven by others. Unexpected events and phenomena often upend our sense of the stable, orderly real world, just as Europeans believed all swans to be white until they saw a black one.

What made Taleb's contribution so timely was the "luck" of a Black Swan event occurring within the financial sector in 2008, only a short time after the book was published. That event was the sudden collapse and bankruptcy of a large, prestigious American financial firm, Lehman Brothers. This touched off a crisis that led to a global economic downturn, and Taleb's discussion of expert blind spots explained why economists were so oblivious and unprepared for the possibility. The situation contributed to *Black Swan*'s enormous success: between its first publication in 2007 and February 2011, it sold 3 million copies and spent 36 weeks on the *New York Times* best seller list. Over the past eight years, it has been translated into 32 languages.[2]

Limitations

Taleb's argument was a thorough and dense explanation of his central idea: that unexpected, potentially random events may occur that have dramatic consequences for the world and our perception of it. But although he discussed this idea in a range of different ways, he found that readers—particularly "professional" thinkers—tried to fit his arguments into familiar boxes. The breadth of Taleb's perspective may have led to this.

In this sense, perhaps *The Black Swan* is only the start of a longer conversation, rather than the definitive statement Taleb expected it to become. However, by opening the door to a range of disciplines for curious onlookers, the book achieved its goal of drawing attention to the significance of Black Swans. On that level, it was a resounding success.

The book is now a familiar presence across a range of disciplines—with the possible exception of economics. Referencing epistemology,* the branch of philosophy concerned with knowledge, Taleb wrote, "Indeed, I am glad at the time of writing, a few years into the life of the book, to see the idea spread among thoughtful readers, inspiring like-minded scholars to go beyond it and seeding research in epistemology, engineering, education, defense, operations research,* statistics,* political theory, sociology,* climate studies,* medicine, law, aesthetics,* and insurance (though not so much in the area in which *The Black Swan* found Black Swan-style near instant vindication, economics)."[3]

NOTES

1 Nassim Nicholas Taleb, *Fooled by Randomness: The Hidden Role of Chance in Life and in the Markets* (London: Penguin, 2007).

2 Charlie Rose, "Charlie Rose talks to Nassim Taleb," Bloomberg Business, February 14, 2011, accessed December 17, 2015, http://www.bloomberg.com/bw/magazine/content/11_10/b4218047676960.htm.

3 Nassim Nicholas Taleb, *The Black Swan: The Impact of the Highly Improbable* (London: Penguin, 2008), 334.

MODULE 8
PLACE IN THE AUTHOR'S WORK

KEY POINTS

- While not a professional philosopher,* Nassim Taleb does a considerable amount of thinking about the role of randomness,* uncertainty, and unpredictability.

- *The Black Swan* represents a middle point in Taleb's writing career, drawing together his earlier thoughts on randomness into a consistent text, from which his later texts emerge to extend the core idea.

- *The Black Swan* became a kind of keystone in the author's four-volume *Incerto* series on the philosophy of uncertainty—although Taleb did not see the book that way before writing it.

Positioning

Before writing *The Black Swan: The Impact of the Highly Improbable*, Nassim Nicholas Taleb had already begun to address the question of uncertainty in his text *Fooled by Randomness: The Hidden Role of Chance in Life and in the Markets* (2001).[1] This book drew on his experience in financial trading,* and the strategies he used to gain large windfalls from essentially random events in the market. *Fooled* was a refreshing addition to the world of popular philosophy. It made less of a dent in the world of academic philosophy, partly because Taleb was not a professional philosopher; his text was therefore written with a voice and style that differed from the established literature of the discipline.

However, *Fooled by Randomness* introduced a range of concepts that Taleb would continue to develop, including the idea of a Black

> **❝** A philosophical essay is a beginning, not an end. To me the very same meditation continues from book to book ... I want my contribution to be a new way of viewing knowledge, the very beginning of a long investigation, the start of something real. **❞**
>
> Nassim Nicholas Taleb, *The Black Swan: The Impact of the Highly Improbable*

Swan itself. Taleb further investigated why the human mind tends to overemphasize and simplify causal relationships;* we tell ourselves stories about what causes things rather than accepting that events can be random.

In *The Black Swan*, Taleb builds on his initial work from the early 2000s. By this stage he had retired from full-time trading and had dedicated himself to exploring his ideas. In *The Black Swan*, he firmly states that we must take the unexpected seriously. Further, he begins to construct a philosophical framework that draws on related developments in fractal geometry,* which looks at patterns that can repeat indefinitely, and chaos theory,* an interdisciplinary study that shows how random events can stem from initial conditions to very different outcomes.

From this alternative perspective on reality, Taleb points to the possibility of protecting against the worst aspects of randomness and uncertainty. He describes the possibility of converting Black Swans into "Gray Swans"*—extreme events that are accounted for in a model. This could contribute to a change in the way economists and other professionals prepare for the future.

However, despite his awareness of the problem of randomness, it was only after the publication of *The Black Swan* that Taleb realized how to combat these threats practically. He suggests in his 2012 book *Antifragile: Things that Gain from Disorder* that the opposite of fragility is not durability, or stability; it is, instead, an openness to change, which converts rapidly moving events into strength rather than weakness.

In 2010, Taleb wrote *The Bed of Procrustes*, a collection of aphorisms,* or short sayings, that contrast certain ways of living and interpreting the world; they are designed to reject what he sees as "nerdiness" and "philistinism" in the modern world[2]—an obsession with technological advances on the one hand, and anti-intellectualism on the other. Again, he deals with similar problems in *Black Swan*, as nerdiness and philistinism can be important factors that get in the way of understanding the nature of the unexpected.

Integration

As a lay philosopher, Taleb believes his ideas hold together and form a single whole. To demonstrate how his thoughts are interconnected, he has combined the four volumes just described into a single title: *Incerto*, from the Latin word for uncertainty. In *Antifragile* Taleb insists, "My writings are not stand-alone essays on specific topics, with beginnings, ends, and expiration dates; rather, they are non-overlapping chapters from that central idea, a main corpus focused on uncertainty, randomness, probability, disorder, and what to do in a world we don't understand."[3]

But how connected or integrated are these volumes? In one sense, they certainly deal with the same themes. Taleb further draws on a range of invented terms across the volumes, which allow complex ideas to be communicated quickly.

Nonetheless, these volumes do not necessarily appear to be equals; not all of them seem necessary contributions to the overall project. *Fooled by Randomness*, for example, exists as a kind of early draft for the more rigorous *The Black Swan*. And *The Bed of Procrustes* is only a collection of aphorisms, which are not required for any particular understanding of Taleb's overall system.

Antifragile, on the other hand, is a robust attempt to apply the theoretical conclusions and consequences of *The Black Swan* to real-life professional practice. If the 2007 *Black Swan* is the "pure" theoretical version of his philosophy, the 2012 *Antifragile* is its "applied" version.

Between *Black Swan* and *Antifragile*, Taleb wrote a range of technical papers and articles in mathematics, philosophy, business, and statistical journals. A more integrated view of his overall work might be found by reading those articles along with the two books themselves. As of late 2015, Taleb was drawing up what he refers to as the mathematical companion to *Incerto*. He calls it *Silent Risk*, and it is available for free in draft form on his website.[4]

Perhaps the author himself is overly invested in what he thinks he has communicated. Readers might not need to digest the entire four-volume series to understand Taleb's ideas on uncertainty.

Significance

Certainly, *The Black Swan* made Taleb's name within intellectual circles and popular readership. His publication of a text about the chance of an unexpected but consequential event was immediately proven relevant when the financial crisis of 2008* drove the market into turmoil. Taleb was immediately offered high-profile interviews, guest lectureships, keynote speeches, and so on. His idea spread far and wide, and his book was soon read around the world.

Luckily, Taleb had been determined to make *The Black Swan* a definitive statement of his philosophical point of view (as it then was). As a result, he showed a level of confidence rarely seen in public intellectual debate.

Although Taleb was not a professional philosopher, he was recognized by academics as someone with an interesting, new, and clear point of view. His ideas were not always understood in full, and he connected them to a wide variety of disciplines; but *The Black Swan* appears to contain the core principles of his philosophy.

NOTES

1   Nassim Nicholas Taleb, *Fooled by Randomness: The Hidden Role of Chance in Life and in the Markets* (London: Penguin, 2007).

2   Nassim Nicholas Taleb, *Bed of Procrustes: Philosophical and Practical Aphorisms* (London: Penguin, 2010).

3   Nassim Nicholas Taleb, *Antifragile: Things That Gain from Disorder* (London: Penguin, 2012).

4   Nassim Nicholas Taleb, *Silent Risk*, accessed December 17, 2015, https://drive.google.com/file/d/0B8nhAlfIk3QIR1o1dnk5ZmRaaGs/view.

SECTION 3
IMPACT

THE FIRST RESPONSES

KEY POINTS

- Several critics of *The Black Swan* appear to have misunderstood Taleb's argument. This resulted in a range of criticisms from economists,* social scientists,* and philosophers* who expected him to help us make better predictions, when his argument was that many predictive models cannot work.

- Other responses were more sympathetic. Statisticians,* for example, welcomed Taleb's explanation regarding the areas of statistics in which their models might work, while exploring the regions where they do not.

- Within the public at large, the early vindication of Taleb's thesis in the financial crisis of 2008* led to widespread interest in his work, which filtered into a range of other disciplines.

Criticism

Several critics said that Nassim Nicholas Taleb's *The Black Swan: The Impact of the Highly Improbable* did not contribute anything new. As Taleb puts it, "This resulted early on in the squeezing of the ideas expressed in *The Black Swan* into a commoditized well-known framework, as if my positions could be squeezed into standard scepticism,* empiricism,* essentialism,* pragmatism,* Popperian falsificationism* … etc."[1]

The public soon began looking more closely at what Taleb had to say. This led to a more rigorous academic response to his ideas on a technical level. Analytic philosophers,* with their

> **❝** A pleasant surprise for me was to discover that the sophisticated amateur who uses books for his own edification, and the journalist ... could understand my idea much better than professionals. Professional readers, less genuine, either read too quickly or have an agenda. **❞**
>
> Nassim Nicholas Taleb, *The Black Swan: The Impact of the Highly Improbable*

emphasis on the scientific and the precise definition of terms, at first mistook his argument for a mere statement of logic—stating the fact that unexpected events can happen—whereas Taleb was keener to examine how these phenomena might occur (and how they might not).

There was a similar misunderstanding among forecasters. Taleb summarizes this as "thinking I am saying 'do not forecast' or 'do not use models' rather than 'do not use sterile forecasts with huge errors.'"[2]

Given his independence from academic discourse (that is, the debates and exchanges that characterize the world of academia) and his popularity with the public, Taleb was able to drive the course of the conversation. He therefore dedicated more attention to constructive criticisms, or discussions that met him on his own terms. One considerable example of this occurred in the field of statistics.

Responses

In August 2007, very shortly after *The Black Swan* was published, the journal *The American Statistician* prepared a special issue to review Taleb's arguments comprehensively.[3] Despite the fact that Taleb had quite dramatically criticized statisticians, the journal was overwhelmingly positive regarding the book's message and purpose. As the reviewers mention, "Despite the numerous irritating comments peppered throughout, the book is quite engaging, well-written, and tells an interesting story."[4]

The reviewers found few arguments to counter Taleb's central idea. In fact, statistics teachers constantly struggle to alert students to the significance of outliers,* or results that are far from those expected. Certain types of statisticians even focus primarily on outliers since they, like Taleb, consider Black Swans to be the most interesting types of data. Economists and others often misuse the principles of the Gaussian bell curve,* and statisticians want to remedy that as much as Taleb does. In fact, they appeared to appreciate the fact that Taleb drew attention to the problems of probability, which is, after all, their main focus of interest.

Conflict and Consensus
Based on the positive and welcoming response from professional statisticians, Taleb was invited to contribute an article. He opted not to irritate this group further. Instead, he offered a friendly explanation for his new concept of dividing decisions based on statistics into "four quadrants."*[5] A decision falls into a quadrant based on whether it is simple or complex, and whether or not a single unexpected event could have a large, consequential effect on the outcome. Taleb told the statisticians, "Your knowledge works beautifully in these three quadrants, but beware of the fourth one, as this is where the Black Swans breed."[6] The fourth quadrant combines complexity with the potential for dramatic consequences.

Soon statisticians began using Taleb's idea of the four quadrants, which identified which regions of reality are "safe," "extremely safe," "sort of safe," and which are Black Swan territory. "That is where the problem resides; opportunities are present too."[7]

From this initial recognition within the world of statistics, Taleb's work began receiving more serious and broad consideration within mathematics, as well as within the fields of complex systems analysis[*] and business studies. Taleb was invited to round table discussions for national security strategies and a range of other topics.

These conversations led in one direction—toward greater technical refinement of his ideas. But Taleb grew wary of the extent to which the world had still not adopted sufficient skepticism.[*]

NOTES

1   Nassim Nicholas Taleb, *The Black Swan: The Impact of the Highly Improbable* (London: Penguin, 2008), 333.

2   Taleb, *Black Swan*, 332.

3   Robert Lund, "Revenge of the White Swan," *American Statistician* 61, no. 3 (2007): 189–92; Peter H. Westfall and Joseph M. Hilbe, "*The Black Swan*: Praise and Criticism," *American Statistician* 61, no. 3 (2007): 193–4.

4   Westfall and Hilbe, "*The Black Swan*: Praise and Criticism," 193–4.

5   Nassim Nicholas Taleb, "Errors, Robustness, and the Fourth Quadrant," *International Journal of Forecasting* 25, no. 4 (2009): 744–59.

6   Taleb, *Black Swan*, 336.

7   Taleb, *Black Swan*, 365.

MODULE 10
THE EVOLVING DEBATE

KEY POINTS

- *The Black Swan*'s recognition of radical contingency* (that is, uncertainty based on possible events) has contributed to a range of fields. It increasingly influences the way some philosophers,* social and natural scientists, and engineers think about certain environmental problems.

- Due to the popularity of the book, Taleb has a widespread and committed following; these devotees are not concentrated within any one academic field and do not amount to a "school" of thought as such.

- The book has not influenced economics* as far as Taleb hoped, but the principles of uncertainty have been integrated into a range of disciplines and discourses due to his accessible writing style in *The Black Swan* and other texts.

Uses and Problems

Nassim Nicholas Taleb's presentation of the limitations of induction* in *The Black Swan: The Impact of the Highly Improbable*, along with the need to recognize the possibility of unpredictable, unforeseen phenomena and events, has influenced a wide range of readers; but these readers are not concentrated in a single discipline. His perspective has been applied to more concrete problems, ranging from national defense to global economic planning. Within these arenas he is regularly brought in as an "outlying voice," and introduced as a critic, rather than as the leader of a new paradigm (that is, a radical new way of interpreting facts).[1]

> ❝ If there is something in nature you don't understand, odds are it makes sense in a deeper way that is beyond your understanding. So there is a logic to natural things that is much superior to our own. Just as there is a dichotomy in law: 'innocent until proven guilty' as opposed to 'guilty until proven innocent,' let me express my rule as follows: what Mother Nature does is rigorous until proven otherwise; what humans and science do is flawed until proven otherwise. ❞
>
> Nassim Nicholas Taleb, *Antifragile: Things That Gain from Disorder*

This led Taleb to develop the more practical aspects of the Black Swan idea in his 2012 book *Antifragile: Things that Gain from Disorder*. Here he expresses his notion that the opposite of fragility is not necessarily durability. Rather, organizations or predictions that stand the test of time are those that can accommodate—and indeed gain from—the natural variations in a chaotic world. Those who make extensive preparations based on the lessons of history may be doomed when the next threat takes a different form. A classic example was the Maginot Line* constructed by France after World War I.* Having felt they had learned from the successes and failures of that war, the French prepared for World War II* in the 1930s by heavily fortifying their border with Germany. But when conflict came, the Germans simply bypassed the frontier from the north, making the entire Maginot Line project a waste of time and effort.

Schools of Thought

Perhaps it is too soon to say, but so far Taleb's influence on academic or philosophical discourse does not seem to be comprehensive or organized—despite his immense popularity among the educated public. While Taleb is known and regularly makes appearances at universities and conferences, no school of thought has consolidated around his work.

In part, this can be attributed to the quirky independence of the author's thought, which still incorporates a wide range of interdisciplinary insights from fields ranging from chaos theory* to fractal geometry.* Because Taleb's perspective is linked to multiple disciplines in nontraditional ways, the interested scholar would have to commit to a wide range of literature to investigate or extend his thinking in any depth.

In other words, Taleb remains a bit of a lone wolf. This does not, however, mean his work has not influenced certain subjects, such as statistics* and mathematics. Some scholars have used his ideas to reinforce their own assumptions about uncertainty, which had previously been undermined through overreliance on the traditional statistical modeling of the Gaussian bell curve.*

At the same time, Taleb has coauthored a range of texts with scholars in the fields of complexity studies* (which explores behaviors within and between systems that can appear to be random) and mathematics. This has added a technical refinement to the perspectives he presented in a more familiar style in *The Black Swan*.

In Current Scholarship

One field in which Taleb's perspective has encountered controversy is ecology. His argument against trusting models appears to fall right into the hands of climate change* skeptics who feel, despite overwhelming evidence, that the science on global warming is not settled.

Taleb distrusts the ecological models, but not because he believes global warming or environmental destruction is not happening. Rather, he feels that because we do not know how, where, or why we are causing this destruction, we should be wary of quick fixes. If scientific evidence is converted too quickly into immediate and dramatic technological remedies, we may distort the environment to an even greater degree. He writes, "We need to be hyper-conservationists ecologically, since we do not know what we are harming with now."[2]

Taleb and his coauthors have made a similar argument about food containing genetically modified organisms* (GMOs).[3] They argue that because we cannot know the full consequences of a potential Black Swan emerging from changes to the genetic coding of vegetables and other foodstuffs, we should reconsider our rush to produce these innovative agricultural products.

Taleb's position on climate change and GMOs has led to widespread criticism from ecological activists and scholars within these fields. They point out, for example, that crossbreeding techniques have been used for millennia, and have entailed similar risks. Taleb suggests these traditional practices are time-tested and therefore "safe," despite being similar in concept to changes made in laboratory conditions using genetic technologies.

NOTES

1   Nassim Nicholas Taleb, *The Black Swan: The Impact of the Highly Improbable* (London: Penguin, 2008), 316.

2   Taleb, *Black Swan*, 125.

3   Nassim Nicholas Taleb et al., "The Precautionary Principle (with Application to the Genetic Modification of Organisms)," Extreme Risk Initiative—NYU School of Engineering Working Paper Series, accessed December 17, 2015, http://arxiv.org/pdf/1410.5787.pdf.

MODULE 11
IMPACT AND INFLUENCE TODAY

KEY POINTS

- *The Black Swan* introduced the problems of uncertainty and improbability to a wide readership. In so doing, the notion of a Black Swan entered public discussion and influenced a range of perspectives on the world we live in.

- While Taleb drew attention to the problems of predictive models, particularly those used in financial* and economic* disciplines, these fields have yet to adjust their practices and methods to accommodate Taleb's ideas in full.

- Taleb's involvement in other fields, including environmentalism, has led to criticism by those who believe his preventative and defensive strategy is "too little too late" with respect to problems such as climate change.*

Position

The central group of scholars that Nassim Nicholas Taleb took issue with in *The Black Swan: The Impact of the Highly Improbable* was economists. He claimed that overreliance on certain forms of statistical modeling made their predictions little better than a soothsayer's warning. Forecasts of economists regularly fail because they rely on a flawed Gaussian curve* distribution method of statistical analysis, which only works in a normal, stable environment. Frighteningly, we continue to return to the same economists again and again for financial and economic predictions. Taleb writes, "Even priests don't go to bishops when they feel ill: their first stop is the doctor's. But we stop by the offices of many

> **❝ At the time of writing, the economics
> establishment is still ignorant of the presence of
> complexity, which degrades predictability. ❞**
>
> Nassim Nicholas Taleb, *The Black Swan: The Impact of the Highly Improbable*

pseudoscientists and experts without alternative. We no longer believe in papal infallibility; we seem to believe in the infallibility of the Nobel, though,"[1] referring to the Nobel Prize in economics.

Taleb was quite disappointed that economists failed to consider or integrate his ideas: "I've debated many economists who claim to specialize in risk and probability: when one takes them slightly outside their narrow focus, but within the discipline of probability, they fall apart, with the disconsolate face of a gym rat in front of a gangster hit man."[2]

However, despite failing to influence his intended target, Taleb did encourage a range of scholars in multiple disciplines, along with the public at large, to take seriously the possibility of the radically contingent*—that is, random events. Taleb's criticism of economists was soon validated by the financial crisis of 2008.* Regardless of this seemingly "hard proof," to this day economists have not addressed Taleb's Black Swan idea in their predictive models.

Interaction

Despite being rejected by the field of economics, *The Black Swan* did receive interest from other disciplines including statistics* and, later, ecological and climate science.* Taleb found himself invited to a range of lectures and panels when his book was followed shortly afterward by the 2008 financial crisis. "Like parties, a book puts you on the envelope of serendipity; it even gets you invited to more parties," he wrote.[3]

However, at first *The Black Swan* was treated like a pop "idea book," the type of philosophical musing one might pick up in an airport bookstore. This led to complaints that the book lacked philosophical rigor. Taleb insisted that his ideas were thorough and that, although he presented them in an informal style, his positions were defensible within the field of epistemology,* the study of the limits and nature of knowledge.

He set out to work through the ideas with more technical specificity, obtaining visiting academic positions at the University of Massachusetts-Amherst, Oxford University, and other institutions. Taleb began to be taken more seriously, and was able to defend his position at both the popular and elite academic level. Meanwhile, the *American Statistician* journal published a comprehensive review of *The Black Swan*, to which Taleb was invited to respond.[4] Though Taleb had been quite critical of statistics in his book, the journal concluded, "At the foundation, Taleb is on our side. We statisticians have fought an uphill battle—forever—to inject probabilistic thinking into daily enterprise … if the end result of the publication of *The Black Swan* is that the general public becomes more aware of the importance of randomness in all areas of human, societal, government, and scientific enterprise, then Taleb will have done the statistical profession a great service."[5]

The Continuing Debate

Since its publication, then, The Black Swan has gradually expanded its reach and significance from the public into the academic world. As Taleb has further refined the technical aspects of his position, he has developed a more formal model of the "fourth quadrant"*—a statistical model designed to show more precisely where we should look out for Black Swans and where we can safely avoid worrying about them.[6] In a revised edition of *The Black Swan* in 2010, Taleb's substantial epilogue provides an explanation of this fourth quadrant idea, as well as the backstory of how the criticisms and discussions he has had since 2007 have contributed to the work's development and extension.[7]

Subsequently, Taleb has also intervened in the field of environmentalism by arguing that our approach to climate change may reflect poor modeling. This does not necessarily mean that we should do nothing, but rather that we should not simply do "something" for the sake of it: we must make sure our interventions do not do more harm than good. Similarly, Taleb and collaborators have argued against experimentation with genetically modified foods* on the grounds that these may lead to a Black Swan event with unfortunate consequences.

Business and organization studies scholars wanted Taleb to suggest practical responses to the uncertainty described in *The Black Swan*. His response is the book *Antifragile: Things That Gain from Disorder*, which suggests that we should not try to make things less fragile by solidifying and reinforcing existing structures; we should, rather, determine how to make those structures more responsive to the changes created by the chaotic world in which we live.[8]

NOTES

1   Nassim Nicholas Taleb, *The Black Swan: The Impact of the Highly Improbable* (London: Penguin, 2008), 291.

2   Nassim Nicholas Taleb, *Antifragile: Things That Gain from Disorder* (London: Penguin, 2012), 242.

3   Taleb, *Black Swan*, 308.

4   Robert Lund, "Revenge of the White Swan," *American Statistician* 61, no. 3 (2007): 189–92; Peter H. Westfall and Joseph M. Hilbe. "*The Black Swan*: Praise and Criticism," *American Statistician* 61, no. 3 (2007): 193–4.

5   Westfall and Hilbe, "*The Black Swan*: Praise and Criticism," 194.

6   Nassim Nicholas Taleb, "Errors, Robustness, and the Fourth Quadrant," *International Journal of Forecasting* 25, no. 4 (2009): 744–59.

7   Taleb, *Black Swan*, 361–73.

8   Taleb, *Antifragile*.

MODULE 12
WHERE NEXT?

KEY POINTS

- Although academia may be slow to change, many scholars are coming to recognize the significance of Taleb's ideas.

- Because of the book's popularity, particularly within practical and professional circles, its ideas may prove useful in the way future social activities are organized.

- Though the text did not introduce many truly new ideas, Taleb did draw together an impressive range of perspectives to support one single-minded message: beware of, and be prepared for, the unexpected.

Potential

Published in 2007, Nassim Nicholas Taleb's *The Black Swan: The Impact of the Highly Improbable* introduced the issues involved in unpredictable and unforeseen events to a wide audience. Although the book is not even a decade old, it has gained widespread popularity and has many supporters across a range of intellectual and professional fields, including statistics,* organization studies* (the study of human organizations), and philosophy.*

While Taleb's ideas may not be completely original, he did popularize and demystify the complex issues of chaos theory* and fractal geometry* (two disciplines that have also challenged notions of certainty), and showed how these relate to the limitations of induction.* These concepts have been around for decades; they had obtained some popular recognition, but were nowhere near as influential as Taleb's work.

Taleb also coins a number of new terms in his writing, including

> ❝Rather than pretend that we can forecast the future, a more intelligent response is to reinforce the resilience of those parts of the financial system that we cannot permit to fail and encourage entry and exit in a free market in other parts. It is clear that we need to understand more about how stability affects risk-taking, leverage, and the 'cycle of confidence'.❞
>
> Professor Sir Meryvn King, Governor of the Bank of England

"the ludic fallacy"* (describing our faith in experts who apply the principles of regulated games, such as those played in casinos, to a reality that actually has no similar constraints at all), the "fourth quadrant"* (the statistical area in which Black Swans would exist), and others. Indeed, even the term "Black Swan" is now widely recognized as a stand-in for any consequential, yet unforeseen, event or phenomenon.

The book's message has now entered the public consciousness. The public has a growing awareness of how important it is to prepare for unforeseen risks, and will increasingly hold public figures to account when they fail to expect the (catastrophically) unexpected. For this reason, *The Black Swan* seems likely to become and remain a classic, as Taleb's ideas are extended and put into practice.

Future Directions

While no school of thought has grown up around Taleb's ideas, he is nonetheless very influential—increasingly so in business and management studies, as well as in organization studies. This influence grew sharply after Taleb's follow-up book, *Antifragile*, was published in 2012. It applied many of the conclusions of *The Black Swan* and suggested practical strategies for creating "non-fragile" institutions.[1]

If organizations are constructed in such a way that they are open to Black Swan events, rather than closed to them, they will be more likely to thrive in a world full of them. One application of this principle is the *Universa* fund, an investment firm that specializes in preparing for and benefiting from Black Swan events. Taleb is an advisor to the fund, which has made tremendous financial gains—up to $1 billion in a single day[2]—by making many small bets against the market, any one of which could soar on the wings of a Black Swan.

Antifragile also influenced the then-governor of the Bank of England, Mervyn King.* While trying to learn from the mistakes of the 2008 crisis, King and others recognized the validity of some of Taleb's ideas. Once these were converted into a practical strategy for avoidance, institutions like the Bank of England could leave themselves less open to dramatic, unforeseen events. They learned that too much "stability" is not necessarily a virtue.

As Taleb put it, "My dream is to have a true Epistemocracy—that is, a society robust against expert errors, forecasting errors, and hubris,* one that can be resistant to the incompetence of politicians, regulators, economists, central bankers, bankers, policy wonks and epidemiologists."*[3] (Epidemiologists are scientists who study epidemics; "hubris" is an extreme form of self-confidence.)

Summary

Taleb's *Black Swan* is well worth reading. It introduces a complex set of ideas in a compelling and easy manner, yet the issues underneath are deep and consequential. These are questions and concerns that we too often ignore due to the very processes that Taleb describes. Our minds do not encourage us to be prepared for Black Swans. Even worse, experts tasked with providing us with safe analyses of potential risks fall into the same trap that we nonexperts make ourselves.

Taleb's work provides an accessible, literary means of coming to terms with these issues. He tells us about the significant findings of several complicated (and sometimes opaque) academic and philosophical fields in an easy-to-understand way.

When reading *The Black Swan*, we wake up to how we are being tricked all the time—by experts and by reality itself. The first step toward freeing ourselves from the worst consequences of Black Swans is awareness. Taleb has made us conscious of these unknowns at every level, from our everyday experiences to the statistical models of experts. By offering us tools to recognize and adapt to the unknown, he has provided an admirable intellectual service.

NOTES

1   Nassim Nicholas Taleb, *Antifragile: Things That Gain from Disorder* (London: Penguin, 2012).

2   Juliet Chung, "A 'Black Swan' fund makes $1 Billion," *Wall Street Journal*, August 30, 2015, accessed December 17, 2015, http://www. wsj.com/articles/nassim-talebs-black-swan-fund-made-1-billion-this-week-1440793953.

3   Nassim Nicholas Taleb, *The Black Swan: The Impact of the Highly Improbable* (London: Penguin, 2008), 322.

GLOSSARIES

GLOSSARY OF TERMS

Aesthetics: a branch of philosophy that addresses art, beauty, and taste, including the way artistic judgments are made and how art is appreciated.

Analytic philosophy: a branch of philosophy popular in English-speaking countries that seeks to address philosophical problems through precise logical statements. Many analytic philosophers equate valid knowledge with the scientific method.

Aphorism: a form of writing that communicates profound, meaningful ideas in a terse, short form, usually a single sentence.

Asymmetric causality: a cause can be symmetric (reversible), or asymmetric and irreversible. The asymmetry reflects the permanence of the new condition—once an asymmetric cause has occurred, it is impossible to go back to the former state. The discovery of a black swan was an asymmetric cause, as it made it impossible to go back to the idea that all swans are white.

Behavioral economics: a field of economics that examines the psychological and social influences on the economic decisions of individuals.

Causal relations: a relationship, or set of relationships, between cause and effect as analyzed using a given theory or set of assumptions.

Chaos theory: an interdisciplinary field of study that is interested in dynamic, actively changing systems, particularly the way in which initial conditions can lead to very different outcomes.

Though developed in mathematics, the theory has influenced not only natural science, but also humanistic scholarship.

Climate change: a change in the overall statistical distribution of weather patterns, as opposed to a simple short-term change in the weather. The most notable recent form of climate change is global warming, in which high concentrations of carbon dioxide emissions appear to be causing a long-term rise in global temperatures.

Cognitive fallacy: a bias that reflects a systematic pattern of departure from what would be considered "rational" reasoning. There are many types of cognitive fallacies, including confirmation bias, ignorance of information, and incorrect distinctions.

Complexity studies: an interdisciplinary field of studies that understands the relationships between parts and the overall system structure as well as interactions with the environment. Complexity science explores behaviors within and between systems that can appear to be random.

Confirmation bias: a psychological bias in which we seek out evidence that confirms our theories, while ignoring or downplaying inconvenient evidence that might disprove our beliefs.

Contingency: phenomena and propositions that depend on the facts of a specific situation, since they are neither true nor false at all times and in all places; rather, they are true depending on the outcome of a given process, or on factual information.

Deductive reasoning: the process of coming to conclusions that are the logical extension of given premises, or principles. If the premises are true, the conclusion must be true.

Economics: a social science that studies the production, distribution, and consumption of goods and services.

Empiricism: the philosophical position that the experience of the senses is the only or primary way in which we can acquire knowledge.

Epistemology: the branch of philosophy interested in the limits or scope of knowledge. Epistemology wants to understand how we can know and justify our knowledge.

Essentialism: the belief that there is something at the core of everything—whether an idea or object—that is vital, or essential, to making it what it is.

Falsificationism: an epistemological principle that considers the successive falsification of theories as a means of identifying that which is not true. This is in contrast to verificationism, which is interested in confirming the validity of true statements.

Finance: the field of study interested in the dynamics of money and investments under conditions of varying uncertainty.

Financial crisis of 2008: after a period of excessive mortgage lending to borrowers who could not afford the payments, in 2008 the entire financial system seemed about to collapse, leading to the largest crisis since the catastrophic economic downturn of the late 1920s and 1930s known as the Great Depression. Several large banks and insurance companies were threatened, including Lehman Brothers, which went bankrupt.

Fourth quadrant: a term invented by Taleb to describe the statistical region in which Black Swans exist. It is the complex region of radical uncertainty, which is inherently unknowable.

Fractal geometry: the study of fractals, which are mathematical sets that repeat the same pattern infinitely. There is no limit to the smallness or largeness of a fractal set. These mathematical principles can be used to examine natural phenomena that also have repeating patterns.

Gaussian curve/bell curve: a statistical model named after the mathematician Carl Friedrich Gauss, who discovered the mathematical function represented by a symmetrical "bell curve" shape. Also known as the "normal distribution," the Gaussian graph bulges toward the middle of a statistical plot, reflecting the concentration of averages. It then declines, tailing off equally on both sides.

Genetically modified organisms: organisms in which elements of DNA have been intentionally altered to produce desirable outcomes. Applied in the realm of food, these modifications may produce a longer shelf life or better taste, but are controversial due to the fact that the technology is relatively new and, perhaps, not fully tested.

Gray Swans: Black Swans that can be partially accounted for, such as earthquakes or stock market shocks, but which cannot be completely known in terms of precise calculations.

Hubris: extreme pride or self-confidence.

Hurricane Katrina: a hurricane that struck the Atlantic seaboard of the United States in 2005, resulting in the deaths of 1,245 people.

Inductive reasoning: a form of reasoning that seeks evidence in support of a given conclusion rather than absolute proof (which can be found through deductive reasoning). An inductive conclusion is probable (rather than certain), since further evidence could theoretically change the conclusion.

Lebanese Civil War: a conflict that started suddenly in Lebanon in 1975 and lasted until 1990. The fighting was among a wide range of different parties including Christians and Muslims, both Shia and Sunni.

Logical positivism/positivism: positivism is a philosophical position related to empiricism, asserting that natural phenomena provide valid, positive knowledge. This implies that sense experience of natural phenomena is the only authoritative base for knowledge. The term positivism was coined in the mid-1800s, but later adopted by logical positivists, who believed the logic of the scientific method should form the basis for other forms of knowledge.

Ludic fallacy: a term invented by Taleb to describe our faith in experts who apply the principles of a regulated game (such as those played in casinos) to reality. This leads to overconfidence in certain probability models, giving them game-like probabilities, when in fact reality is not subject to the same regulations as games.

Maginot Line: a line of concrete fortifications constructed during the 1930s by the French along the border with Germany.

Narrativity: the manner in which stories, or narratives, are presented and reinforced in the mind. The "narrative fallacy" is the tendency to settle on a story to explain events and phenomena, and then to disregard evidence that does not fit the narrative.

Ontology: the branch of philosophy interested in existence, or being.

Operations research: an academic discipline dealing with decision-making using advanced analytical methods. Also known as management science.

Organization studies: the study of human organizations, interested both in the organization as such and in human behavior within the organization. It draws on psychology, economics, sociology, anthropology, and related disciplines.

Outlier: a statistical observation, or data point, that is far removed from the other results in a statistical plot.

Philosophy: as an academic discipline, philosophy is interested in fundamental questions of existence, knowledge, reason, language, and related ideas. It addresses problems in a systematic way, probing these fundamental questions for deeper answers, or to introduce new problems. It is broken into many subfields, including ontology, aesthetics, metaphysics, epistemology, and so on.

Postmodernism: a cultural and philosophical movement of the late twentieth century that encouraged a radical break with the principles of modernism, which in turn had rejected the ideas of the past. Postmodernists emphasize a skeptical orientation to culture, including art, architecture, and criticism, emphasizing contingency and the relative nature of knowledge.

Pragmatism: a philosophical tradition that emerged in the United States in the 1870s, which rejected the notion that thought should necessarily mirror reality. Rather, pragmatism claims that our minds are engaged in predictions, problem-solving, and practical action and that our beliefs, knowledge, and meaning are dependent on these practical activities, their successes, and their failures.

Randomness: the absence of pattern or predictability in sequences of events.

Risk analysis: an approach or technique for assessing how likely it is that a project or undertaking will succeed or fail, and the factors that may affect this.

Scientism: belief in the universal applicability of the scientific method.

Skepticism: a philosophical distrust of any knowledge or opinions that are stated as fact. Skeptics require empirical evidence before they will believe unsubstantiated claims.

Sociology: the scientific study of human and social behavior, with general interests in social order and social change, and specific interests in social stratification, deviance, ideology, and many other related concerns.

Statistics: a field of study interested in the collection, organization, and analysis of data using numerical representations of things.

Systems analysis: an approach that looks at how all the different parts of a system fit together to make it work, with the aim of improving the system's function and efficiency.

Trader: in finance, a person or firm that buys and sells stocks, bonds, commodities, and other financial instruments.

Wall Street crash of 1987: refers to Monday 19, 1987, when stock markets around the world crashed, starting with the stock market on Wall Street in New York. This resulted in a huge loss of value.

World War I: a war lasting from 1914 to 1918 and principally a conflict between the Austro-Hungarian and German empires on one side and the British, French and Russian empires on the other. The nations initially involved all had complex systems of alliances and, as a result, many states around the world entered into the conflict, resulting in around 20 million deaths.

World War II: usually dated from 1939 to 1945, although conflict between China and Japan started before that. Like World War I, what started as a European conflict between Germany and her neighbors resulted in the eruption of tensions around the world and about 50 million deaths before it was brought to an end.

PEOPLE MENTIONED IN THE TEXT

Thomas Friedman (b. 1953) is an American journalist and author who writes on topics related to global affairs, including economic and national security issues. He was influential in popularizing the idea of globalization for a wide public audience.

Carl Friedrich Gauss (1777–1855) was a German mathematician who developed a range of mathematical techniques, the most well known of which is the Gaussian curve, or "normal distribution."

Malcolm Gladwell (b. 1963) is a Canadian author, who worked at the *New Yorker* before becoming a bestselling writer of popular books, including *The Tipping Point* and *Outliers*. These introduced readers to interesting, thought-provoking ideas without using a lot of academic jargon.

David Hume (1711–76) was a Scottish philosopher who contributed to the Scottish Enlightenment (a period of European intellectual history in which ideas of rationality and liberty came to prominence) with his radical empiricism, skepticism, and naturalism.

Benoit Mandelbrot (1924–2010) was a Polish French American mathematician who invented the field of fractal geometry.

Robert C. Merton (b. 1944) is an American economist and Nobel laureate who codeveloped the Black-Merton-Scholes formula, a technique used to measure and reduce risk within financial investments.

Karl Popper (1902–94) was an Austrian British philosopher of science who rejected the classical inductivist model of the scientific method in favor of an empirical, falsificationist position.

Adolph Quetelet (1796–1874) was a Belgian statistician influential in introducing statistical techniques to the study of society.

Myron Scholes (b. 1941) is an American economist and Nobel laureate who codeveloped the Black-Merton-Scholes formula, a technique used to measure and reduce risk within financial investments.

WORKS CITED

WORKS CITED

Chung, Juliet. "A 'Black Swan' fund makes $1 Billion." *Wall Street Journal*, August 30, 2015. Accessed December 17, 2015. http://www.wsj.com/articles/nassim-talebs-black-swan-fund-made-1-billion-this-week-1440793953.

Hacking, Ian. *Logic of Statistical Inference*. Cambridge: Cambridge University Press, 1965.

Hume, David. *A Treatise of Human Nature: Being an Attempt to Introduce the Experimental Method of Reasoning into Moral Subjects*. Oxford: Oxford University Press, 2000.

Kahneman, Daniel and Amos Tversky. "On the Reality of Cognitive Illusions," *Psychological Review* 103, no. 3 (1996): 582–91.

Lowenstein, Roger. *When Genius Failed: The Rise and Fall of Long-Term Capital Management.* New York: Random House, 2000.

Lund, Robert. "Revenge of the White Swan." *American Statistician* 61, no 3 (2007): 189–92.

Mandelbrot, Benoit. *The Fractal Geometry of Nature*. New York: W.H. Freeman and Co., 1982.

Moon, Francis. *Chaotic and Fractal Dynamics*. New York: Wiley, 1992.

Piketty, Thomas. *Capital in the Twenty-First Century*. Translated by Arthur Goldhammer. Cambridge, MA: Harvard University Press, 2014.

Popper, Karl. *The Logic of Scientific Discovery*. 15th Edition. London: Routledge, 2002.

Rose, Charlie. "Charlie Rose talks to Nassim Taleb." Bloomberg Business, February 14, 2011. Accessed December 17, 2015. http://www.bloomberg.com/bw/magazine/content/11_10/b4218047676960.htm.

Taleb, Nassim Nicholas. *Fooled by Randomness: The Hidden Role of Chance in Life and in the Markets*. London: Penguin, 2007.

— — —. *The Black Swan: The Impact of the Highly Improbable*. London: Penguin, 2008.

— — —. "Errors, Robustness, and the Fourth Quadrant." *International Journal of Forecasting* 25, no. 4 (2009): 744–59.

— — —. *The Bed of Procrustes: Philosophical and Practical Aphorisms*. London: Penguin, 2010.

————. *Antifragile: Things That Gain from Disorder*. London: Penguin, 2012.

————. *Silent Risk*. Accessed December 17, 2015. https://drive.google.com/file/d/0B8nhAlfIk3QIR1o1dnk5ZmRaaGs/view.

Taleb, Nassim Nicholas, and Constantine Sandis. "The Skin in the Game Heuristic for Protection Against Tail Events." *Review of Behavioral Economics* 1 (2014): 1–21.

Taleb, N. N., R. Read, R. Douady, J. Norman, and Y. Bar-Yam. "The Precautionary Principle (with Application to the Genetic Modification of Organisms)." Extreme Risk Initiative—NYU School of Engineering Working Paper Series. Accessed December 17, 2015. http://arxiv.org/pdf/1410.5787.pdf.

Westfall, Peter H., and Joseph M. Hilbe. "*The Black Swan*: Praise and Criticism." *American Statistician* 61, no. 3 (2007): 193–4.

THE MACAT LIBRARY
BY DISCIPLINE

AFRICANA STUDIES

Chinua Achebe's *An Image of Africa: Racism in Conrad's Heart of Darkness*
W. E. B. Du Bois's *The Souls of Black Folk*
Zora Neale Huston's *Characteristics of Negro Expression*
Martin Luther King Jr's *Why We Can't Wait*
Toni Morrison's *Playing in the Dark: Whiteness in the American Literary Imagination*

ANTHROPOLOGY

Arjun Appadurai's *Modernity at Large: Cultural Dimensions of Globalisation*
Philippe Ariès's *Centuries of Childhood*
Franz Boas's *Race, Language and Culture*
Kim Chan & Renée Mauborgne's *Blue Ocean Strategy*
Jared Diamond's *Guns, Germs & Steel: the Fate of Human Societies*
Jared Diamond's *Collapse: How Societies Choose to Fail or Survive*
E. E. Evans-Pritchard's *Witchcraft, Oracles and Magic Among the Azande*
James Ferguson's *The Anti-Politics Machine*
Clifford Geertz's *The Interpretation of Cultures*
David Graeber's *Debt: the First 5000 Years*
Karen Ho's *Liquidated: An Ethnography of Wall Street*
Geert Hofstede's *Culture's Consequences: Comparing Values, Behaviors, Institutes and Organizations across Nations*
Claude Lévi-Strauss's *Structural Anthropology*
Jay Macleod's *Ain't No Makin' It: Aspirations and Attainment in a Low-Income Neighborhood*
Saba Mahmood's *The Politics of Piety: The Islamic Revival and the Feminist Subject*
Marcel Mauss's *The Gift*

BUSINESS

Jean Lave & Etienne Wenger's *Situated Learning*
Theodore Levitt's *Marketing Myopia*
Burton G. Malkiel's *A Random Walk Down Wall Street*
Douglas McGregor's *The Human Side of Enterprise*
Michael Porter's *Competitive Strategy: Creating and Sustaining Superior Performance*
John Kotter's *Leading Change*
C. K. Prahalad & Gary Hamel's *The Core Competence of the Corporation*

CRIMINOLOGY

Michelle Alexander's *The New Jim Crow: Mass Incarceration in the Age of Colorblindness*
Michael R. Gottfredson & Travis Hirschi's *A General Theory of Crime*
Richard Herrnstein & Charles A. Murray's *The Bell Curve: Intelligence and Class Structure in American Life*
Elizabeth Loftus's *Eyewitness Testimony*
Jay Macleod's *Ain't No Makin' It: Aspirations and Attainment in a Low-Income Neighborhood*
Philip Zimbardo's *The Lucifer Effect*

ECONOMICS

Janet Abu-Lughod's *Before European Hegemony*
Ha-Joon Chang's *Kicking Away the Ladder*
David Brion Davis's *The Problem of Slavery in the Age of Revolution*
Milton Friedman's *The Role of Monetary Policy*
Milton Friedman's *Capitalism and Freedom*
David Graeber's *Debt: the First 5000 Years*
Friedrich Hayek's *The Road to Serfdom*
Karen Ho's *Liquidated: An Ethnography of Wall Street*

John Maynard Keynes's *The General Theory of Employment, Interest and Money*
Charles P. Kindleberger's *Manias, Panics and Crashes*
Robert Lucas's *Why Doesn't Capital Flow from Rich to Poor Countries?*
Burton G. Malkiel's *A Random Walk Down Wall Street*
Thomas Robert Malthus's *An Essay on the Principle of Population*
Karl Marx's *Capital*
Thomas Piketty's *Capital in the Twenty-First Century*
Amartya Sen's *Development as Freedom*
Adam Smith's *The Wealth of Nations*
Nassim Nicholas Taleb's *The Black Swan: The Impact of the Highly Improbable*
Amos Tversky's & Daniel Kahneman's *Judgment under Uncertainty: Heuristics and Biases*
Mahbub Ul Haq's *Reflections on Human Development*
Max Weber's *The Protestant Ethic and the Spirit of Capitalism*

FEMINISM AND GENDER STUDIES

Judith Butler's *Gender Trouble*
Simone De Beauvoir's *The Second Sex*
Michel Foucault's *History of Sexuality*
Betty Friedan's *The Feminine Mystique*
Saba Mahmood's *The Politics of Piety: The Islamic Revival and the Feminist Subject*
Joan Wallach Scott's *Gender and the Politics of History*
Mary Wollstonecraft's *A Vindication of the Rights of Women*
Virginia Woolf's *A Room of One's Own*

GEOGRAPHY

The Brundtland Report's *Our Common Future*
Rachel Carson's *Silent Spring*
Charles Darwin's *On the Origin of Species*
James Ferguson's *The Anti-Politics Machine*
Jane Jacobs's *The Death and Life of Great American Cities*
James Lovelock's *Gaia: A New Look at Life on Earth*
Amartya Sen's *Development as Freedom*
Mathis Wackernagel & William Rees's *Our Ecological Footprint*

HISTORY

Janet Abu-Lughod's *Before European Hegemony*
Benedict Anderson's *Imagined Communities*
Bernard Bailyn's *The Ideological Origins of the American Revolution*
Hanna Batatu's *The Old Social Classes And The Revolutionary Movements Of Iraq*
Christopher Browning's *Ordinary Men: Reserve Police Batallion 101 and the Final Solution in Poland*
Edmund Burke's *Reflections on the Revolution in France*
William Cronon's *Nature's Metropolis: Chicago And The Great West*
Alfred W. Crosby's *The Columbian Exchange*
Hamid Dabashi's *Iran: A People Interrupted*
David Brion Davis's *The Problem of Slavery in the Age of Revolution*
Nathalie Zemon Davis's *The Return of Martin Guerre*
Jared Diamond's *Guns, Germs & Steel: the Fate of Human Societies*
Frank Dikotter's *Mao's Great Famine*
John W Dower's *War Without Mercy: Race And Power In The Pacific War*
W. E. B. Du Bois's *The Souls of Black Folk*
Richard J. Evans's *In Defence of History*
Lucien Febvre's *The Problem of Unbelief in the 16th Century*
Sheila Fitzpatrick's *Everyday Stalinism*

Eric Foner's *Reconstruction: America's Unfinished Revolution, 1863-1877*
Michel Foucault's *Discipline and Punish*
Michel Foucault's *History of Sexuality*
Francis Fukuyama's *The End of History and the Last Man*
John Lewis Gaddis's *We Now Know: Rethinking Cold War History*
Ernest Gellner's *Nations and Nationalism*
Eugene Genovese's *Roll, Jordan, Roll: The World the Slaves Made*
Carlo Ginzburg's *The Night Battles*
Daniel Goldhagen's *Hitler's Willing Executioners*
Jack Goldstone's *Revolution and Rebellion in the Early Modern World*
Antonio Gramsci's *The Prison Notebooks*
Alexander Hamilton, John Jay & James Madison's *The Federalist Papers*
Christopher Hill's *The World Turned Upside Down*
Carole Hillenbrand's *The Crusades: Islamic Perspectives*
Thomas Hobbes's *Leviathan*
Eric Hobsbawm's *The Age Of Revolution*
John A. Hobson's *Imperialism: A Study*
Albert Hourani's *History of the Arab Peoples*
Samuel P. Huntington's *The Clash of Civilizations and the Remaking of World Order*
C. L. R. James's *The Black Jacobins*
Tony Judt's *Postwar: A History of Europe Since 1945*
Ernst Kantorowicz's *The King's Two Bodies: A Study in Medieval Political Theology*
Paul Kennedy's *The Rise and Fall of the Great Powers*
Ian Kershaw's *The "Hitler Myth": Image and Reality in the Third Reich*
John Maynard Keynes's *The General Theory of Employment, Interest and Money*
Charles P. Kindleberger's *Manias, Panics and Crashes*
Martin Luther King Jr's *Why We Can't Wait*
Henry Kissinger's *World Order: Reflections on the Character of Nations and the Course of History*
Thomas Kuhn's *The Structure of Scientific Revolutions*
Georges Lefebvre's *The Coming of the French Revolution*
John Locke's *Two Treatises of Government*
Niccolò Machiavelli's *The Prince*
Thomas Robert Malthus's *An Essay on the Principle of Population*
Mahmood Mamdani's *Citizen and Subject: Contemporary Africa And The Legacy Of Late Colonialism*
Karl Marx's *Capital*
Stanley Milgram's *Obedience to Authority*
John Stuart Mill's *On Liberty*
Thomas Paine's *Common Sense*
Thomas Paine's *Rights of Man*
Geoffrey Parker's *Global Crisis: War, Climate Change and Catastrophe in the Seventeenth Century*
Jonathan Riley-Smith's *The First Crusade and the Idea of Crusading*
Jean-Jacques Rousseau's *The Social Contract*
Joan Wallach Scott's *Gender and the Politics of History*
Theda Skocpol's *States and Social Revolutions*
Adam Smith's *The Wealth of Nations*
Timothy Snyder's *Bloodlands: Europe Between Hitler and Stalin*
Sun Tzu's *The Art of War*
Keith Thomas's *Religion and the Decline of Magic*
Thucydides's *The History of the Peloponnesian War*
Frederick Jackson Turner's *The Significance of the Frontier in American History*
Odd Arne Westad's *The Global Cold War: Third World Interventions And The Making Of Our Times*

LITERATURE

Chinua Achebe's *An Image of Africa: Racism in Conrad's Heart of Darkness*
Roland Barthes's *Mythologies*
Homi K. Bhabha's *The Location of Culture*
Judith Butler's *Gender Trouble*
Simone De Beauvoir's *The Second Sex*
Ferdinand De Saussure's *Course in General Linguistics*
T. S. Eliot's *The Sacred Wood: Essays on Poetry and Criticism*
Zora Neale Huston's *Characteristics of Negro Expression*
Toni Morrison's *Playing in the Dark: Whiteness in the American Literary Imagination*
Edward Said's *Orientalism*
Gayatri Chakravorty Spivak's *Can the Subaltern Speak?*
Mary Wollstonecraft's *A Vindication of the Rights of Women*
Virginia Woolf's *A Room of One's Own*

PHILOSOPHY

Elizabeth Anscombe's *Modern Moral Philosophy*
Hannah Arendt's *The Human Condition*
Aristotle's *Metaphysics*
Aristotle's *Nicomachean Ethics*
Edmund Gettier's *Is Justified True Belief Knowledge?*
Georg Wilhelm Friedrich Hegel's *Phenomenology of Spirit*
David Hume's *Dialogues Concerning Natural Religion*
David Hume's *The Enquiry for Human Understanding*
Immanuel Kant's *Religion within the Boundaries of Mere Reason*
Immanuel Kant's *Critique of Pure Reason*
Søren Kierkegaard's *The Sickness Unto Death*
Søren Kierkegaard's *Fear and Trembling*
C. S. Lewis's *The Abolition of Man*
Alasdair MacIntyre's *After Virtue*
Marcus Aurelius's *Meditations*
Friedrich Nietzsche's *On the Genealogy of Morality*
Friedrich Nietzsche's *Beyond Good and Evil*
Plato's *Republic*
Plato's *Symposium*
Jean-Jacques Rousseau's *The Social Contract*
Gilbert Ryle's *The Concept of Mind*
Baruch Spinoza's *Ethics*
Sun Tzu's *The Art of War*
Ludwig Wittgenstein's *Philosophical Investigations*

POLITICS

Benedict Anderson's *Imagined Communities*
Aristotle's *Politics*
Bernard Bailyn's *The Ideological Origins of the American Revolution*
Edmund Burke's *Reflections on the Revolution in France*
John C. Calhoun's *A Disquisition on Government*
Ha-Joon Chang's *Kicking Away the Ladder*
Hamid Dabashi's *Iran: A People Interrupted*
Hamid Dabashi's *Theology of Discontent: The Ideological Foundation of the Islamic Revolution in Iran*
Robert Dahl's *Democracy and its Critics*
Robert Dahl's *Who Governs?*
David Brion Davis's *The Problem of Slavery in the Age of Revolution*

Alexis De Tocqueville's *Democracy in America*
James Ferguson's *The Anti-Politics Machine*
Frank Dikotter's *Mao's Great Famine*
Sheila Fitzpatrick's *Everyday Stalinism*
Eric Foner's *Reconstruction: America's Unfinished Revolution, 1863-1877*
Milton Friedman's *Capitalism and Freedom*
Francis Fukuyama's *The End of History and the Last Man*
John Lewis Gaddis's *We Now Know: Rethinking Cold War History*
Ernest Gellner's *Nations and Nationalism*
David Graeber's *Debt: the First 5000 Years*
Antonio Gramsci's *The Prison Notebooks*
Alexander Hamilton, John Jay & James Madison's *The Federalist Papers*
Friedrich Hayek's *The Road to Serfdom*
Christopher Hill's *The World Turned Upside Down*
Thomas Hobbes's *Leviathan*
John A. Hobson's *Imperialism: A Study*
Samuel P. Huntington's *The Clash of Civilizations and the Remaking of World Order*
Tony Judt's *Postwar: A History of Europe Since 1945*
David C. Kang's *China Rising: Peace, Power and Order in East Asia*
Paul Kennedy's *The Rise and Fall of Great Powers*
Robert Keohane's *After Hegemony*
Martin Luther King Jr.'s *Why We Can't Wait*
Henry Kissinger's *World Order: Reflections on the Character of Nations and the Course of History*
John Locke's *Two Treatises of Government*
Niccolò Machiavelli's *The Prince*
Thomas Robert Malthus's *An Essay on the Principle of Population*
Mahmood Mamdani's *Citizen and Subject: Contemporary Africa And The Legacy Of Late Colonialism*
Karl Marx's *Capital*
John Stuart Mill's *On Liberty*
John Stuart Mill's *Utilitarianism*
Hans Morgenthau's *Politics Among Nations*
Thomas Paine's *Common Sense*
Thomas Paine's *Rights of Man*
Thomas Piketty's *Capital in the Twenty-First Century*
Robert D. Putman's *Bowling Alone*
John Rawls's *Theory of Justice*
Jean-Jacques Rousseau's *The Social Contract*
Theda Skocpol's *States and Social Revolutions*
Adam Smith's *The Wealth of Nations*
Sun Tzu's *The Art of War*
Henry David Thoreau's *Civil Disobedience*
Thucydides's *The History of the Peloponnesian War*
Kenneth Waltz's *Theory of International Politics*
Max Weber's *Politics as a Vocation*
Odd Arne Westad's *The Global Cold War: Third World Interventions And The Making Of Our Times*

POSTCOLONIAL STUDIES

Roland Barthes's *Mythologies*
Frantz Fanon's *Black Skin, White Masks*
Homi K. Bhabha's *The Location of Culture*
Gustavo Gutiérrez's *A Theology of Liberation*
Edward Said's *Orientalism*
Gayatri Chakravorty Spivak's *Can the Subaltern Speak?*

PSYCHOLOGY

Gordon Allport's *The Nature of Prejudice*
Alan Baddeley & Graham Hitch's *Aggression: A Social Learning Analysis*
Albert Bandura's *Aggression: A Social Learning Analysis*
Leon Festinger's *A Theory of Cognitive Dissonance*
Sigmund Freud's *The Interpretation of Dreams*
Betty Friedan's *The Feminine Mystique*
Michael R. Gottfredson & Travis Hirschi's *A General Theory of Crime*
Eric Hoffer's *The True Believer: Thoughts on the Nature of Mass Movements*
William James's *Principles of Psychology*
Elizabeth Loftus's *Eyewitness Testimony*
A. H. Maslow's *A Theory of Human Motivation*
Stanley Milgram's *Obedience to Authority*
Steven Pinker's *The Better Angels of Our Nature*
Oliver Sacks's *The Man Who Mistook His Wife For a Hat*
Richard Thaler & Cass Sunstein's *Nudge: Improving Decisions About Health, Wealth and Happiness*
Amos Tversky's *Judgment under Uncertainty: Heuristics and Biases*
Philip Zimbardo's *The Lucifer Effect*

SCIENCE

Rachel Carson's *Silent Spring*
William Cronon's *Nature's Metropolis: Chicago And The Great West*
Alfred W. Crosby's *The Columbian Exchange*
Charles Darwin's *On the Origin of Species*
Richard Dawkin's *The Selfish Gene*
Thomas Kuhn's *The Structure of Scientific Revolutions*
Geoffrey Parker's *Global Crisis: War, Climate Change and Catastrophe in the Seventeenth Century*
Mathis Wackernagel & William Rees's *Our Ecological Footprint*

SOCIOLOGY

Michelle Alexander's *The New Jim Crow: Mass Incarceration in the Age of Colorblindness*
Gordon Allport's *The Nature of Prejudice*
Albert Bandura's *Aggression: A Social Learning Analysis*
Hanna Batatu's *The Old Social Classes And The Revolutionary Movements Of Iraq*
Ha-Joon Chang's *Kicking Away the Ladder*
W. E. B. Du Bois's *The Souls of Black Folk*
Émile Durkheim's *On Suicide*
Frantz Fanon's *Black Skin, White Masks*
Frantz Fanon's *The Wretched of the Earth*
Eric Foner's *Reconstruction: America's Unfinished Revolution, 1863-1877*
Eugene Genovese's *Roll, Jordan, Roll: The World the Slaves Made*
Jack Goldstone's *Revolution and Rebellion in the Early Modern World*
Antonio Gramsci's *The Prison Notebooks*
Richard Herrnstein & Charles A Murray's *The Bell Curve: Intelligence and Class Structure in American Life*
Eric Hoffer's *The True Believer: Thoughts on the Nature of Mass Movements*
Jane Jacobs's *The Death and Life of Great American Cities*
Robert Lucas's *Why Doesn't Capital Flow from Rich to Poor Countries?*
Jay Macleod's *Ain't No Makin' It: Aspirations and Attainment in a Low Income Neighborhood*
Elaine May's *Homeward Bound: American Families in the Cold War Era*
Douglas McGregor's *The Human Side of Enterprise*
C. Wright Mills's *The Sociological Imagination*

Thomas Piketty's *Capital in the Twenty-First Century*
Robert D. Putman's *Bowling Alone*
David Riesman's *The Lonely Crowd: A Study of the Changing American Character*
Edward Said's *Orientalism*
Joan Wallach Scott's *Gender and the Politics of History*
Theda Skocpol's *States and Social Revolutions*
Max Weber's *The Protestant Ethic and the Spirit of Capitalism*

THEOLOGY

Augustine's *Confessions*
Benedict's *Rule of St Benedict*
Gustavo Gutiérrez's *A Theology of Liberation*
Carole Hillenbrand's *The Crusades: Islamic Perspectives*
David Hume's *Dialogues Concerning Natural Religion*
Immanuel Kant's *Religion within the Boundaries of Mere Reason*
Ernst Kantorowicz's *The King's Two Bodies: A Study in Medieval Political Theology*
Søren Kierkegaard's *The Sickness Unto Death*
C. S. Lewis's *The Abolition of Man*
Saba Mahmood's *The Politics of Piety: The Islamic Revival and the Feminist Subject*
Baruch Spinoza's *Ethics*
Keith Thomas's *Religion and the Decline of Magic*

COMING SOON

Chris Argyris's *The Individual and the Organisation*
Seyla Benhabib's *The Rights of Others*
Walter Benjamin's *The Work Of Art in the Age of Mechanical Reproduction*
John Berger's *Ways of Seeing*
Pierre Bourdieu's *Outline of a Theory of Practice*
Mary Douglas's *Purity and Danger*
Roland Dworkin's *Taking Rights Seriously*
James G. March's *Exploration and Exploitation in Organisational Learning*
Ikujiro Nonaka's *A Dynamic Theory of Organizational Knowledge Creation*
Griselda Pollock's *Vision and Difference*
Amartya Sen's *Inequality Re-Examined*
Susan Sontag's *On Photography*
Yasser Tabbaa's *The Transformation of Islamic Art*
Ludwig von Mises's *Theory of Money and Credit*